C. G. Jung

The Fundamentals of Theory and Practice

C. G. Jung
The Fundamentals of Theory and Practice

Elie G. Humbert

Translated by Ronald G. Jalbert

Chiron Publications
Wilmette, Illinois

Fourth printing, 1996

Originally published in 1984 as C. G. *Jung*
Copyright 1983, Editions Universitaires, Paris

Translation © 1988 by Chiron Publications
Library of Congress Catalog Card Number: 88-2582

Edited by Priscilla Coit Murphy
Book design by Kirk George Panikis
Printed in the United States of America

Library of Congress Cataloging-in-Publication Data

Humbert, Elie G.
  [C.G. Jung. English]
  C.G. Jung : the fundamentals of theory and practice / Elie G. Humbert.
    p.   cm.
  Translation of: C.G. Jung.
  Bibliography: p.
  Includes index.
  ISBN 978-0-933029-18-7
    1. Jung, C. G. (Carl Gustav), 1875–1961. 2. Psychoanalysis.
  I. Title.
  BF173.J85H8313   1988   88-2582
  150.19′54—dc19   CIP

The world into which we are born is brutal and cruel, and at the same time of divine beauty. Which element we think outweighs the other, whether meaninglessness or meaning, is a matter of temperament. If meaninglessness were absolutely preponderant, the meaningfulness of life would vanish to an increasing degree with each step in our development. But that is—or seems to me—not the case. Probably, as in all metaphysical questions, both are true: life is—or has—meaning and meaninglessness. I cherish the anxious hope that meaning will preponderate and win the battle.

—Carl G. Jung, *Memories, Dreams, Reflections*

Contents

PART TWO

Reflections on the Relations Between
Consciousness and the Unconscious

Translator's Preface

Paris 1928—*le Groupe d'Etudes C.G. Jung* is founded. The formation of this study group marks the beginning of organized French interest in Jungian psychology. In a brief yet informative historical overview of the Jungian presence in Paris, Jean Clausse quotes Suzanne Percheron, who interviewed Jung in 1957. Jung told her: "What matters is that Paris have its own group and that you teach there everything I have been able to teach you" (*Le Groupe d'Etudes C.G. Jung* in a reprint from the *Cahiers de Psychologie Jungienne*, no. 18, 1978, p. 8). Jung felt strongly that Paris had to keep his psychology alive and well. The threat in those early years and later was that analytical psychology would be completely overshadowed by the Freudians, and that Jung's thought would be seen at best as a curiosity, an oddity not deserving of the attention of the serious student or of the professional. Through much perseverance and effort, including that of many outstanding analytical psychologists, the French training society, the *Société Française de Psychologie Analytique*, was finally founded in 1969.

It is fitting that Elie Humbert's book is the first by a major French Jungian analyst to be translated into English, since Elie Humbert is a significant contributor to the Jungian presence not only in Paris but throughout France. Elie Humbert is a co-founder of the *Société*, where he has been a well-respected teacher and mentor since the mid-60s. He began analytic training in 1957, when he met regularly with Jung. These meetings continued until Jung's health began to deteriorate the year before his death. It is known that Jung held a high opinion of his French student's intellectual abilities and psychological sensitivity. Elie Humbert is among the last of the first-generation analysts, that is, those analysts trained by Jung himself. During 1974 and 1975, Humbert was called upon to function as the president of the French Jung Society. In 1974, he was instrumental in starting the highly respected Jungian journal, the *Cahiers de Psychologie Jungienne*, now known as the *Cahiers Jungiens de Psychanalyse*, where he has been editor-in-chief since its beginnings.

Elie Humbert's influence in the French intellectual world is extensive. The present book on Jung is considered a major reference source in France. He is the only Jungian analyst to have enjoyed the privilege of teaching psychology at the University of Paris VII, a renowned bastion of Freudian thought.

The present volume is a synthesis of Elie Humbert's personal reflections on Jung's works and analytic approach. It demonstrates his unusual ability to distill a vast amount of information, grasp the essence of an analytic concept, and express it incisively and concisely. When he entertains other currents of thought, it is to use the terminology of the ambient intellectual world as a foil for furthering his own thought. He rethinks many current analytic concepts from the perspective of his own personal and clinical experience while remaining faithful to the framework of Jung's methodology and theory.

The author is noted for a style that combines a highly refined clinical sensitivity with a philosophical sophistication in epistemology, the latter having been a passion among most analytic schools in France, particularly since Lacan. One of the outstanding features of this book, aside from its substantive contributions to Jungian thought, is its philosophical, psychological, and clinical sophistication. The author is clearly as adept at tackling thorny epistemological questions as he is at making clinically relevant suggestions.

One purpose of this book is to engage the reader in re-examining Jungian concepts within the broad outlines of the Jungian tradition. This means taking on Jung's *method*—which leads to a confrontation with the unconscious, his *epistemology*—which articulates that confrontation, and his *clinical work*—which demonstrates the impact of the unconscious upon the dialectical relationship between analyst and analysand. A thorough grasp of these three areas demands an in-depth knowledge of Jung's works, an awareness of one's own psyche, and much clinical experience. There is no doubt that the author of the present book excels in all three areas.

In order to appreciate more fully the kind of book Elie Humbert has written and its uniqueness, it is well worth the effort to reflect briefly on the nature of analytic writing.

Jung tells us that psychological writing is always a confession about the writer's own psychology. Elie Humbert adds that it is a continuation of one's own analysis. It is in both of these senses, as confession and as continuation of analysis, that this book bears a stamp of lyricism while remaining scientific, in the best tradition of psychological writing. It is clear that the paths he outlines are those he has traveled. One assurance that the author has assimilated the psychological realities he discusses lies in the manner in which he expresses those realities.

The author's language is not simply that of the professional or the academic. The ideas conveyed are technical, certainly. Every word was weighed, but weighed as the words of a poem are weighed by the poet, in an effort to create an effect, to invite the reader to experience the unconscious and to reflect on that experience.

Psychological experience is an experience in language, as Jung first demonstrated in his word-association experiments. Jung recognized this truth, even if he was later to turn from the language of words to the language of images. If psychological writing is a confession for the writer, it is also no less a confession of sorts for the reader who takes in the writer's words, who is touched by and identifies with what is said. The reader's experience is to witness the potential unfolding of his or her inner life in the writer's confession of personal psychological experiences.

If one takes into consideration two dimensions of analytical writing, the mythic and the scientific, one has to agree that psychological writing cannot restrict itself to the limits imposed by empirical science. This view is opposed to one trend in the clinical field that strives toward procedures and techniques that are so generalizable that they exclude the individuality of the therapist. Techniques and procedures become primary while the person of the therapist is virtually "factored out." This book stands in marked contrast to that trend.

Those uninitiated to Jung's thought will find here an excellent guide to many of Jung's basic concepts. But the author not only introduces us to Jung's concepts, he also initiates us into the basics of Jung's method— a phenomenological one, and into Jung's epistemologies. The book is an encounter with the unconscious and an invitation to readers to plumb further their own depths. The relationship with the unconscious is to be as alive and actual as the relationship between the analyst and the analysand. Thus the book can be counted among those rare works in analytic literature that stand on the level with Jung's own writings.

There are several reasons for the great number of direct quotations from Jung's works. First, the reader is enabled to read Jung's own works, to become acquainted with the Jung who persists in his writings. Moreover, it is not uncommon in French writings on a writer's thought to rely more heavily on direct quotations than on paraphrase and indirect references. The integrity of the author's words is respected while allowing the commentator's remarks and observations to highlight the text. Interpretation is already present in the selection of texts. Selection thereby becomes composition, much as a quilt or a collage may form and express a new whole.

One final reason needs to be given for the author's ample use of quotations. He wants the reader to enter into dialogue with Jung's own text, in the same way that he encourages dialogue with the unconscious. The learning of analytic concepts demands that the learner be active.

Since dialogue is fundamental to Elie Humbert's approach to the psyche, this book is intended to enact, symbolically, exactly what it talks about. It is hoped that the reader will react to this book as an invitation to a dialogue with the author.

Acknowledgments

Translator's Acknowledgments

I would like to express my deepest appreciation to the author and his wife, Myrtha, who warmly received me in their home in Paris during an intense and enriching week of reviewing the translation. Their hospitality, trust, intellectual vitality, and kindness nourished body, intellect, and soul.

I also wish to acknowledge the publisher, Murray Stein, for his encouragement throughout the project.

Special thanks go to my wife, Nancy, who listened to several revisions and made suggestions that have become part of the text. She added a decidedly Anglo-Saxon accent to my French one.

Eleanor Irwin read a later draft and raised relevant questions that saved the translator from some embarrassment. A note of appreciation goes to Marcel Gaumond, who helped in cross-checking references, and to Laura Pence, who typed the first draft.

Author's Acknowledgment

The author would like to acknowledge Mrs. Cecile Penette whose editorial assistance during the writing of the original French version was invaluable.

List of Abbreviations

C.W. = *The Collected Works. of C.G. Jung*, trans. R. F. C. Hull, Bollingen Series XX, Vols. 1–14, 16–18. Copyright © by Princeton University Press, Princeton, N.J. For a complete listing, see Index.

G.W. = *Gesmmelte Werke.* Verlag; Osten.

E. = "Entretiens avec C.G. Jung," Suzanne Percheron in *Cahiers de Psychologie Jungienne*, No. 6, 1975.

F/J = *The Freud-Jung Letters*, edited by W. McGuire. Princeton University Press; Princeton, 1974.

H.D.A. = *L'Homme à la Decouverte de son Ame*, translated by R. Cahen. Payot; Paris, 1966.

I.E.M. = *Introduction à l'Essence de Mythologie*, translated by E. del Medico. Payot; Paris, 1953.

I.P. = "Introduction" à la *Psychologie de C.G. Jung* by J. Jacobi, translated by J. Chavy. *Editions du* Mont Blanc; Genève, 1964.

J.L. = *Letters* of C.G. Jung, vols. 1 and 2. Princeton University Press; Princeton, 1973 and 1975.

M.D.R. = *Memories, Dreams, Reflections.* Random House; New York, 1972.

Mét. = *Métamorphoses de l'Ame et ses Symboles*, preface and translation by Y. Le Lay. Buchet-Chastel; Paris, 1953.

P.I. = *Psychologie de l'Inconscient*, preface and translation by R. Cahen. Buchet-Chastel; Paris, 1951.

V.S. = *Vision Seminars*, Books 1 and 2. Spring Publications, Zürich, 1976.

All quotations followed by "tr. RGJ" were translated from the French by the present translator, Ronald G. Jalbert.

Chronology of Jung's Life

1875   Carl Gustav Jung is born July 26 in Kesswil (situated in the Canton of Thurgovia in Switzerland) of Carl Gustav Jung, son of John Paul Achilles (1842–1896), pastor in this parish, and Emily, born Preiswerk (1848–1923).

1879   The Jung family moves to Klein-Huningen, near Basel. Young Carl begins secondary studies at the *Gymnasium* in Basel.

1884   Birth of Jung's sister, Gertrude (death in 1935).

1895–1900   Studies medicine at the University of Basel.

1896   Death of his father on January 28 of this year.

1900   Second assistant to Eugen Bleuler, chief physician at the Burghölzli Klinik, a psychiatric hospital in Zürich.

1902   First assistant at the Burghölzli. Doctoral thesis in medicine, "On the Psychology and Pathology of So-called Occult Phenomena."

1902–1903   Winter semester with Pierre Janet at the Salpétrière.

1903   Marriage to Emma Rauschenbach (1882–1955), resident of Schaffhausen. Together they will have four daughters and one son.

1905–1909   Clinical director at the Burghölzli.

1905–1913   Privatdozent at the Faculty of Medicine of Zürich. Teaches psychology and psychoneurosis.

1907   *The Psychology of Dementia Praecox.* Meets Freud for the first time in Vienna in February.

1908   First International Congress of Psychoanalysis in Salzburg.

1909   Private practice in Küsnacht, 228 Seestrasse. First trip to the United States with Freud and Ferenczi on the occasion of the twentieth anniversary of Clark University.

1909–1913   Editor-in-chief of the *Jahrbuch für psychoanalytische und psychopathologische Forschungen,* founded by Freud and Bleuler.

1910   Second International Congress of Psycholoanalysis, in Nuremburg.

1910–1914   First president of the International Association of Psychoanalysis.

1911   Third International Congress of Psychoanalysis in Weimar.

1912   Conferences on "The Theory of Psychoanalysis" at Fordham University in New York. First edition of *Symbols of Transformation.* Break with Freud.

1913   Fourth International Congress of Psychoanalysis, in Munich. Jung calls his psychology "analytical psychology." Resigns from his teaching post at the University of Zürich.

1914   Gives conferences in London and in Aberdeen. Drafted into the health services.

1916   *Seven Sermons to the Dead*. "The Transcendent Function." Begins the study of gnosticism.

1918–1919   Commander of prisoner-of-war camp for English soldiers in Chateau-d'Oex (Vaud). Discovers importance of painting mandalas.

1920   Trips to Algeria and Tunisia.

1921   *Psychology Types*.

1922   Buys land on the shores of Lake Zürich in the commune of Bollingen.

1923   Builds Bollingen Tower on Lake Zürich. Death of his mother. First conferences given by Richard Wilhem on the *I Ching* at the Zürich Psychology Club.

1924–1925   Travels to the United States, visits the Pueblo Indians of New Mexico.

1925–1926   Expedition to Uganda, Kenya, and along the shores of the Nile. Visits the Elgonyis at Mount Elgon.

1928   "The Relations between the Ego and the Unconscious." "On Psychic Energy."

1929   "Commentary on 'The Secret of the Golden Flower.'"

1930   Vice-president of the General Medical Society for Psychotherapy (E. Kretschmer, President).

1931   *The Psychological Problems of the Present Time*.

1932   Awarded prize in literature by the city of Zürich.

1933   First seminar at the Polytechnical School of the University of Zürich. First conference at Eranos in Ascona. Trip to Egypt and to Palestine.

1934   President of the General Medical Society for Psychotherapy.

1934–1939   Editor-in-chief of the *Zentralblatt für Psychotherapie und ihre Grenzgebiete* (Leipzig).

1935   Professor at the Polytechnical School of the University of Zürich. Founds the Swiss Society for Applied Psychology. Tavistock Lectures in London.

1936   Awarded *doctor honoris causa* at Harvard. "Wotan."

1937   Terry Lectures at Yale.

1938   Voyage to India by invitation of the British government for the twentieth anniversary of the Indian Society of Sciences. President of the International Congress for Psychotherapy at Oxford. *Doctor honoris causa* at Oxford. Fellow of the Royal Society of Medicine.

1939   Resigns from the International Medical Society for Psychotherapy.

1940   Works are inscribed on the Otto list, along with Freud's. *Psychology and Religion.*

1941   *Essays on the Science of Mythology*, with C. Kerenyi.

1942   Resigns from his professorship at the Polytechnical School.

1943   Becomes member of the Swiss Academy of Sciences.

1944   Named chair of the Psychology Department of the Faculty of Medicine of Basel. Resigns the same year for health reasons. *Psychology and Alchemy.*

1945   *Doctor honoris causa* at the University of Geneva.

1946   *Psychology of the Transference. Psychology and Education.*

1948   *Symbols of the Spirit.* Founding of the C.G. Jung Institute in Zürich.

1950   *Formations of the Unconscious.*

1951   *Aion.*

1952   "Synchronicity: An Acausal Connecting Principle." Revision of *Symbols of Transformation. Answer to Job.*

1953   First volume of *The Collected Works* in English, translation by R.F.C. Hull.

1954   *Roots of Consciousness.*

1955   *Doctor honoris causa* at the Polytechnical School of Zürich. Death of his wife on November 27.

1955–1956   *Mysterium Coniunctionis.*

1957   *The Undiscovered Self.* Begins his autobiography with the help of Aniela Jaffé. BBC interview with John Freeman.

1958   *A Modern Myth.* First volume of German edition of the *Collected Works.*

1960   Honorary citizen of Küsnacht.

1961   Ten days before his death, finishes "Approaching the Unconscious," in *Man and his Symbols.* Dies June 6 at his home in Küsnacht.

Introduction

The meaning of life and of words—these were the topics that drew Jung's attention while he worked as a psychiatrist with the mentally ill. Through his clinical experience, Jung learned that ideas have value only to the extent that they are life-promoting. He also came to understand that only by becoming more conscious can one truly tend to one's own psychic ills.

Consciousness is open to the world and to human history, both of which it truly fails to encounter, except where the subject experiences meaninglessness, that is, where the subject feels psychologically wounded. While the process of becoming conscious demands nothing more than increased self-knowledge, it finally touches upon the unknown dimensions of existence itself as much as it involves the particulars of the individual's life history.

The process of becoming conscious has been misunderstood, for it is a difficult one to sustain. Many have embarked upon it as a way of undertaking psychoanalysis while sidestepping its requirements. They have scorned psychoanalysis or allowed themselves to be entertained by it, which would seem to indicate that they have read Jung simply at the content level without understanding the manner in which he dealt with that content. They have failed to see the clinical questions that underlie Jung's references to mythology and alchemy. They have arbitrarily preferred, rather, to relate mythological and alchemical themes to anthropology, religion, or semiology. Zealots and detractors alike delude themselves about psychoanalysis, the one by exaggerated admiration, the other by unfair criticisms.

Jung's writings are analytic texts, which is to say they do not purport to present the conceptual framework of an analytic approach. Instead, they present Jung's own confrontation with the unconscious. Writing played a special role in Jung's life, as it does in the lives of most analytic thinkers. Analytic writing flows from analysts' own self-analysis, which is conducted in counterpoint to the analysis that they do with patients. When analysts write, they project their own psychological investment in analysis and express for themselves the meaning analysis has for them. In so doing, they modify their libidinal economy and give birth to a new metaphor.

In reading Jung, one must keep track of these various dimensions. Those who open one of Jung's books hoping to find a theory of psychology risk being disappointed, for they will likely find in Jung's texts only a mixture of diverse pieces grouped together in a rather confusing way. Readers will fail to grasp the guiding thread of Jung's work if they do not understand that they have entered into the presence of a living encounter with the unconscious.

This is not to claim that the reader will find the "true" Jung in the present book. I did know him personally and worked with him. I also sought to understand myself through his works for more than twenty years. My personal experience of Jung has taught me that Jung is much more than what I can say about him. This book seeks only to give a useful approximation of his work.

My goal is to show how Jung's psychotherapeutic practice and personal reflection interact—how they join and connect. I have noted why this articulation is not so apparent in his written work. It does exist, however; and it takes the form of a consistent approach to psychological material. It is this approach that we will uncover and follow.

The scope of this book demands that I be concise. I have therefore deliberately avoided developing, debating, or discussing theses. For similar reasons, I have decided not to discuss the relationship between Jung's major ideas and other psychoanalytic movements. Jung's work contributes numerous observations and raises many questions that other psychoanalytic schools have ignored. It would be beyond the scope of this work to speak about these schools. In the present study, I have therefore limited myself to the.task of teasing out the internal logic of Jung's own work.

Jung's opus finds its true roots in an intense confrontation with the unconscious, which took place between the years 1912 and 1919. While this period in Jung's life serves as a starting point for this present study, I want to backtrack briefly and show how his work was already germinating and gradually making itself known in the years preceding the 1912–1919 time period.

Two of Jung's principal interests at the beginning of his career are significant for his later work. The first of these is the association experiment; the second concerns mediumistic phenomena. Jung's participation in parapsychological sessions demonstrates how far the range of psychological investigations extends. Jung even devoted his doctoral thesis in medicine to a parapsychological study entitled "On the Psychology and

Pathology of So-Called Occult Phenomena." He was later to propose a theory of the unconscious that would attempt to encompass all irrational phenomena. This theory was to be far-reaching enough to include, for example, the concept of synchronicity.

In 1900, Jung became assistant at the Burghölzli Klinik, a psychiatric hospital in Zürich directed by Eugen Bleuler. There, he passionately devoted himself to the study of the association experiment which Bleuler, his mentor, had initiated. This experiment consisted in presenting a series of stimulus words to a patient and asking the patient to associate to each word, one at a time. Jung then noted the words the patient produced for each stimulus word, the time elapsed before each response, and the manner in which the response was given. Between 1904 and 1909, Jung published enough studies on the association experiment to fill an entire volume of the Collected Works (cf. C.W. 2).

Those word-association experiments led Jung to discover the existence of thought-affect nuclei. Although not directly observable, these nuclei are rigidly structured and interfere with the patient's associations. Jung suggested the term "complex" for these thought-affect nuclei. His earlier research into complexes predisposed Jung to accept the idea of the unconscious when he became acquainted with Freud's works in 1906. More precisely, Freud gave Jung a specifically clinical understanding of the unconscious, one that underscores the role of unconscious formations in everyday life.

A complex consists of a cluster of emotionally charged representations. Upon closer examination, one discovers within the complexes a core element that serves as a vehicle for meaning and that functions independently of conscious will. This core element links together a network of associations that originate either from an innate predisposition or from the individual's experience as it is conditioned by the environment. These associations form a cluster of thought-affect contents, which makes its presence felt in the way it molds behavior into typical patterns. Complexes are caused by traumatic experiences, by repression, or by the impossibility of making certain unconscious factors conscious. Because complexes are loaded with autonomous affective charges, they force consciousness into repetitive patterns. Jung will later add that the structure of the complex is organized according to archetypal schemas and that a conscious understanding of this structure diminishes its repetitive or destructive effects, resulting in a constructive rechanneling of affect.

In the early years of his professional life, Jung devoted his first major work to the study of complexes, *The Psychology of Dementia Praecox* (1907). The title is revealing since it shows that the notion of the complex was well suited to understanding the psychotic patients whom Jung was treating daily. The complex theory explains how the psyche can be fragmented into autonomous forces. It is through the effects of these autonomous forces that the unconscious is experienced. Complexes impose their emotions, images, and orientations upon consciousness. Relative to these, the ego is but one complex, albeit a privileged one, among many others.

In February 1907, Freud invited Jung to Vienna. Their first conversation lasted thirteen hours, and they subsequently maintained a six-year correspondence with each other. Freud and Jung also journeyed to the U.S. together. Still later, Jung became the first president of the International and Psychoanalytic Association. These historical facts demonstrate the importance and the intimacy of their relationship.

During their association, Jung attempted to apply psychoanalysis to the therapy of psychotic patients; and he also undertook a psychoanalytic interpretation of myths. Freud encouraged this twofold development because he hoped that it would lead to a further verification of his own discoveries. But the application of psychoanalytic theory to the therapy of psychotic patients and to the interpretation of myths led Jung to become more and more conscious of how his views differed from Freud's.

During this time, too, Jung observed while analyzing neurotics that children's images of their parents do not simply reflect their actual parents. Jung concluded that the child's image of the parents depends just as much upon the child's psyche as it does upon the parents' real characteristics. To designate the schema that is most properly the child's and that is least reflective of the child's actual parents, Jung coined the term *imago*.

These two ideas, "complex" and "imago," are at the basis of Jung's psychology. The first describes a dynamic perspective permitting understanding of the structural organization of the multiple, autonomous forces confronted by the ego in its efforts toward greater consciousness. The second concept, the "imago," describes the intrapsychic field to the extent that the "object" receives its form and name from the schemas that belong to the subject's own psyche. The concept of imago (*Vorbild*) leads to the concept of archetype (*Urbild*).

Jung's publication of his *Symbols of Transformation* in 1912–13 precipitated his break with Freud. Of all the ideas that Jung drew from his years of collaboration with Freud, the most important was undoubtedly the idea of the unconscious. Even though he understood the unconscious differently from Freud, Jung never questioned its existence.

Toward the end of his life, while reminiscing about the causes of his break with Freud, Jung wrote the following:

> When I was working in my book about the libido and approaching the end of the chapter "The Sacrifice," I knew in advance that its publication would cost me my friendship with Freud. For I planned to set down in it my own conception of incest, the decisive transformation of the concept of libido, and various other ideas in which I differed from Freud. . . . But Freud clung to the literal interpretation of it and could not grasp the spiritual significance of incest as a symbol. (M.D.R., p. 167)

In breaking with Freud, Jung knew that he was trying to preserve his own understanding of the symbol and his conviction that it is possible to have a living relationship with the unconscious. This relationship, he believed, ensues as a result of symbolic incest and sacrifice.

Another matter at stake, however, seems to have remained unconscious for Jung, even though it appears in the evolution of his thought following his break from Freud: the problem of the subject. In fact, in the years immediately following his split from Freud, Jung developed the idea of the Self. At the same time, Freud formulated his theory of narcissism and devised his second topography. The convergence of Freud's and Jung's interest concerning the subject is significant, but their approaches are not easily reconcilable.

At about this same time, Sabina Spielrein asked both Freud and Jung a question, which neither dealt with frankly, and which, perhaps, underscores the radical difference between these two men: Is destruction the cause of becoming?

PART ONE

Confrontation with the Unconscious

Chapter 1

Conscious Activity: Three Verbs

> After the parting of the ways with Freud, a period of inner uncertainty began for me. It would be no exaggeration to call it a state of disorientation. I felt totally suspended in mid-air, for I had not yet found my own footing. (M.D.R., p. 170)

The year is 1912 and Jung was facing the end of an intense relationship with Freud. At thirty-seven years of age, he was enjoying an international reputation; and he had already demonstrated an astounding ability to cast old problems in new forms while laying the foundations for his own work. Now, for example, he was free to dedicate himself to his interest in schizophrenia. But his separation from Freud had thrown him into a state of uncertainty; he was no longer sure of himself.

In this uncertainty Jung still faced the immediate duties to family and patients. Furthermore, he clung firmly to the idea that all of human reality consists of a relationship between consciousness and the unconscious. Indeed, he remained convinced about the existence of an autonomous psychic activity that is non-willed and non-conscious; but he no longer believed all that was said about it. He decided to allow the unconscious to speak and to remain open to what might happen. In short, he gave himself the task of experiencing and learning from his own psyche without relying on any preconceived ideas.

Geschehenlassen (to let happen)

> Thereupon I said to myself, "Since I know nothing at all, I shall simply do whatever occurs to me." (M.D.R., p. 173)

With this attitude of openness, Jung began to play.

> I began accumulating suitable stones, gathering them partly from the lake shore and partly from the water. And I started building; cottages, a castle,

9

a whole village. . . . I went on with my building game after the noon meal every day, whenever the weather permitted. As soon as I was through eating, I began playing, and continued to do so until the patients arrived; and if I finished with my work early enough in the evening, I went back to building. . . . I had no answer to my question, only the inner certainty that I was on the way to discovering my own myth. For the building game was only a beginning. (M.D.R., pp. 174–5)

Jung uses the word *geschehenlassen* ("to let happen") to describe the way in which he deals with whatever comes to mind. *Geschehenlassen* is noteworthy, for it combines the passive and the active meanings of *lassen* (to allow, to let and to cause, to effect) with *geschehen* (to happen, to occur, to take place), the latter suggesting different ways in which events appear to consciousness. The German verb *geschehenlassen*, however, connotes neither a state of abandon, within which anything could emerge, nor a passive sort of "letting go."

Indeed, it is not sufficient to "let oneself go" with whatever presents itself to consciousness, because the urge to seek immediate satisfaction to the wishes that arise tends to drown out the more profound voices that emanate from inner orientations and desires. One may ask how one is to distinguish deep inner inclinations from mere impulses and daydreaming. One must, in a certain way, give birth to the unconscious, one must "make it happen." Nothing is heard when one takes the path of least resistance.

It was during Advent of the year 1913—December 12, to be exact—that I resolved upon the decisive step. I was sitting at my desk once more, thinking over my fears. Then I let myself drop. Suddenly, it was as though the ground literally gave way beneath my feet, and I plunged down into the depths. I could not fend off a feeling of panic. (M.D.R., p. 179)

Can one give free reign to unconscious impulses without paying a price? Does one not risk destroying others and oneself? When engaged in transposing fantasies and affects into concrete forms, is there not the danger that one will be overwhelmed by them and be drawn into acting them out?

Betrachten (to consider, to impregnate)

Faced with emerging psychic phenomena, Jung's text does not lend itself to analytic schemas, but rather relies upon the importance of paying attention. Jung takes upon himself the tasks of objectifying and considering the emerging unconscious.

Betrachten means "to consider." We could translate the word with the expression "to realize" as it is used in its intransitive meaning, which de-notes the act of becoming aware of the existence of something other than oneself. Jung's use of the term *betrachten* implies allowing the power of what is unknown within the unconscious to manifest itself without be-coming possessed by it. "To realize" consists here of objectifying affects or impulses. When one feels caught in one's moods or caught up by ready-made ideas, one generally seeks to be rid of them by using inter-pretations and judgments, which in the final analysis are simply other moods and other opinions. Is one not better off writing about them or drawing pictures of them?

> Had I left those images hidden in the emotions, I might have been torn to pieces by them. There is a chance that I might have succeeded in splitting them off; but in that case I would inexorably have fallen into a neurosis and so been ultimately destroyed by them anyway. (M.D.R., p. 177)

> I made a beginning by writing down the fantasies which had come to me during my building game. This work took precedence over everything else. An incessant stream of fantasies had been released. . . . (M.D.R., p. 176)

Subjects can disentangle and differentiate themselves from the emo-tions and impulses that affect them by objectifying these emotions and impulses and, in this way, by relating to them.

> The German *betrachten*. . . also means "to make pregnant." *Trächtig* means to be pregnant, carrying young, but it is used only for animals, not for hu-man beings. So to look at or concentrate upon an object conveys to it the quality of pregnancy. And if it is pregnant, it is alive, it produces, it multiplies. That is the case with any phantasy image. One concentrates on it, then finds difficulty in keeping it quiet; it gets restless, it shifts; some-thing is added to it or it multiplies itself; one fills it with living power and it becomes pregnant. . . . (V.S., p. 260)

The same thing happens to subjects since they also can be psychologi-cally impregnated by an image. But the forces that give life to the im-pregnated subject threaten to take their own course and to keep for themselves what could become a fertile power.

Betrachten also means to put oneself at a distance. *Betrachtung* corre-sponds to the Greek *Theoria*, which simultaneously means contemplation and the idea that results from contemplation. This activity is scientific to the extent that science consists of a process of objectification which alters the subject.

Such objectification rarely occurs at the beginning of analysis. For quite a while in analysis, it is the analyst who has to exercise the *Betrachten* and who, in this way, gradually makes possible a transformation in the analysand's field of consciousness. The analytic session carves out from everyday time a privileged moment during which anything can be said and considered.

Sich auseinandersetzen (to confront oneself with)

Distancing oneself from whatever happens as one confronts the unconscious, and considering it without any preconceptions, creates a tension widening a gap between consciousness and the unconscious. Within this space, the unconscious manifests itself as much through events as through the passions that are filtered through moods and ideas. The subject engaging in such a confrontation with the unconscious becomes conscious. At the same time, the manifestations of the unconscious become more powerful and more elemental.

> An incessant stream of fantasies had been released, and I did my best not to lose my head but to find some way to understand these strange things. I stood helpless before an alien world; everything in it seemed difficult and incomprehensible. I was living in a constant state of tension; often I felt as if gigantic blocks of stone were tumbling down upon me. . . . My enduring these storms was a question of brute strength. Others have been shattered by them. . . . But there was a demonic strength in me, and from the beginning there was no doubt in my mind that I must find the meaning of what I was experiencing in these fantasies. (M.D.R., pp. 176–7)

The human need for meaning is not merely intellectual. If Jung sought to understand the fantasies that welled up in him, it was to understand their impact upon his life. Within such a confrontation, consciousness presents itself as "subject" and recognizes the unconscious as "other." That is to say, the unconscious presents itself as an autonomous power that forces itself upon the subject and demands to be reckoned with.

> I took great care to try to understand every single image, every item of my psychic inventory, and to classify them scientifically—so far as this was possible—and, above all, to realize them in actual life. That is what we usually neglect to do. We allow the images to rise up, and maybe we wonder about them, but that is all. We do not take the trouble to understand them, let alone draw ethical conclusions from them. This stopping-short conjures up the negative effects of the unconscious.
>
> It is equally a grave mistake to think it is enough to gain some understanding of the images and that knowledge can here make a halt. Insight into them must be converted into an ethical obligation. Not to do so is to fall prey to the power principle. . . . (M.D.R., pp. 192–3)

The ethical question that Jung raised about images is not derived from a moral code or established values. The decision to allow the unconscious to produce what it will transcends these moral considerations. On the other hand, however, the images that well up from the unconscious call the subject into question. The subject can choose either to ignore the unconscious or to let himself be possessed by it. The subject might elect to live a fragmented life rather than to make the necessary effort to confront the unconscious. In any case, neither attitude is without consequence. Nothing can do away with the fact that the subject has experienced these unconscious images and that a meaning might have taken shape had the subject been more receptive to the stirrings of the unconscious.

These three German verbs *geschehenlassen, betrachten,* and *sich auseinandersetzen* together define conscious activity in its confrontation with the unconscious. They set forth the conditions necessary for the experience of the psyche—that experience from which Jung developed his analytic psychology and to which, therefore, one must return if one is to understand what he has written about it.

One year before his death, Jung wrote about his experiences in the following way:

> All my works, all my creative activity, has come from those initial fantasies and dreams which began in 1912, almost fifty years ago. . . . (M.D.R., p. 192)

> The years when I was pursuing my inner images were the most important in my life—in them everything essential was decided. (M.D.R., p. 199)

In order to take stock of what happened during this period of Jung's life, I refer the reader to three of Jung's texts: *The Transcendent Function* (C.W. 8), an essay written in 1916 but not published until 1957; *The Commentary on the Secret of the Golden Flower,* written in 1929 (C.W. 13); and chapter 6 of *Memories, Dreams, Reflections,* which is a reworking of a seminar that Jung gave in 1925 but dictated later, between 1957 and 1959.

Chapter 2

Dreams and Active Imagination

Seeing that at least half of our psychic existence is passed in that [unconscious] realm, and that consciousness acts upon our nightly life just as much as the unconscious overshadows our daily life, it would seem all the more incumbent on medical psychology to sharpen its senses by a systematic study of dreams. Nobody doubts the importance of conscious experience; why then should we doubt the significance of unconscious happenings? They also are part of our life, and sometimes more truly a part of it for weal or woe than any happenings of the day. (C.W. 17, par. 325)

One can, while awake, allow the unconscious to speak, notably through the use of free association and of active imagination but "the dream is specifically the utterance of the unconscious." (C.W. 17, par. 317)

Dreams

Jung describes how, after his break from Freud, he returned once more to analyzing dreams and fantasies.

Above all, I felt it necessary to develop a new attitude toward my patients. I resolved for the present not to bring any theoretical premises to bear upon them, but to wait and see what they would tell of their own accord. My aim became to leave things to chance. The result was that the patients would spontaneously report their dreams and fantasies to me, and I would merely ask, "What occurs to you in connection with that?" or, "How do you mean that, where does that come from, what do you think about it?" The interpretations seemed to follow of their own accord from the patients' replies and associations. I avoided all theoretical points of view and simply helped the patients to understand the dream images by themselves, without application of rules and theories. (M.D.R., p. 170)

As his work progressed, Jung used his knowledge of psychic processes to interpret dreams and fantasy material. He always insisted, however, that the unconscious remains "unconscious" and that one must look to

each dream in view of learning something new and not for the mere purpose of finding within it the confirmation of what one already knows.

> As soon as a certain "monotony of interpretation" strikes us, we know that
> our approach has become doctrinaire and hence sterile. (M.D.R., p. 312)

The Language of Images

In 1907, in his book *The Psychology of Dementia Praecox,* Jung relied
upon his clinical experience to challenge Freud's idea that censorship
must necessarily be at the origin of dreams. He maintained, nonetheless,
a position that comes close to Freud's when he wrote in the first version
of *Symbols of Transformation* in 1911: "Dreams are symbolic so that we
may not understand them, in order that desire, the source of the dream,
may not be understood" (Mét., p. 127, tr. RGJ).

From 1913 on, Jung rejected this suspicious interpretation, which he
believed reflected an unfounded prejudice. He preferred to see dreams as
"natural phenomena," a hypothesis that he felt was theoretically most
frugal and which he hoped might prove most fruitful.

> To me, dreams are a part of nature, which harbors no intention to de-
> ceive, but expresses something as best it can, just as a plant grows or an
> animal seeks its food as best it can. (M.D.R., pp. 161–2)

This is not to suggest that Jung believed that dreams simply or directly
express the unconscious, or that he ignored or rejected Freud's idea of
"dream-work." It must not be forgotten that it was Jung's enthusiastic
reading of Freud's *Traumdeutung* that brought him to Freud in the first
place. Like Freud's theory, Jung's phenomenology of dreams recognized
the processes of displacement, condensation, and symbolization. However, Jung did not believe that these mechanisms are necessarily the result of censorship. He thought, rather, that they belong to the poly-
semous nature of the image.

Jung analyzed at length the polysemy of images in his book *The
Psychology of the Unconscious* (Chapters 6 and 7), where he interpreted
a crab image that appeared in a woman's dream. Among several seem-
ingly unconnected images, the crab image seemed to him to be the best
possible representation of the unconscious link that connects many
"scenes" and other images from the woman's life such as: the embraces
that the woman dreamer relished in her mother's arms and that now
bind her to a woman friend; the cancer that, in her view, punishes the
sensuality of a woman whom she knows; the fear that an artist, a former
lover of the cancerous woman, evokes in her; a certain anxiety that was
transferred from her woman friend and projected on to her analyst.

The image of the crab does not hide anything. On the contrary, it reveals quite precisely the unconscious factor present in the different living situations just mentioned. To understand this unconscious factor, one has to recognize that the crab in the woman's dream is an element of a vocabulary that differs from the conceptual.

> Dreams, then, convey to us in figurative language—that is, in sensuous, concrete imagery—thoughts, judgments, views, directives, tendencies, which were unconscious either because of repression or through mere lack of realization. (C.W. 8, par. 477)

Jung adopted one of Nietzsche's ideas when he stated "that dream-thinking should be regarded as a phylogenetically older mode of thought" (C.W. 8, par. 474). Abstract thought is a relatively recent development in the evolution of psychic "products." The dream's imagistic language is therefore closer to the night world than to the day world.

The language of images is demanding in its own way. If the image makes sense because of its ability to "bind" different meanings together within a given context and to convey a precise intention, it cannot be properly understood unless what "binds" the meanings together is discovered. Those who interpret images are generally tempted to play with the polysemy of images and to slide from one meaning to another. The interpretation of a dream requires, by contrast, that all associations relating to the dream be retained if one is to grasp the unique meaning of a particular dream image. Dream interpretation is a precise task which demands that attention be given to differences and not only to similarities.

The Language of Drama

Dreams generally appear in a dramatic form. Actors enter the dream by relating to each other in the same way as participants in a waking life scene. And these interactions within dreams are meaningful. In order to grasp this meaning, Jung suggested that dreams be interpreted in much the same way as a play. After the first images have set the stage for the unconscious processes that unfold, the drama gathers momentum and develops into plots. It culminates in the climax, the turning point in the dream, from which the finale or *lysis* flows. An analysis of the dramatic structure of the dream allows the interpreter to discern the permutations of the dream elements and to perceive the connection between those elements that appear within the scene and those that disappear from it. Furthermore, this method of dream analysis remains faithful to the associationist idea according to which sequence signifies consequence. The woman's dream of the crab illustrates this idea:

> She is about to cross a wide river. There is no bridge, but she finds a ford where she can cross. She is on the point of doing so, when a large crab that lay hidden in the water seizes her by the foot and will not let her go. (C.W. 7, par. 123)

The association of the dream's images link the crossing of the river with the changes that the dreamer senses she has to make in her life. The dream tells us that there is no bridge to allow for this crossing, only a ford, a situation that suggests to the waking ego that the dreamer should undergo analysis. Within the dream, the dreamer accepts the challenge presented to her and crosses the ford. However, she comes across an unexpected obstacle: the crab that bites her foot. One wonders if she is able to continue. Will becoming conscious of what the crab represents make the crab let go of her foot? The dreamer ends up in an unexpected predicament whose causes are almost entirely unconscious.

The way in which the dream unfolds provides information that we did not have beforehand. In fact, the neurotic nature of the dreamer's relationship to her mother and to her woman friend are evident. Equally obvious is the anxiety-provoking nature of the crab. Nonetheless, only the sequence of images within the dream reveals precisely the dreamer's actual unconscious situation. Without understanding the sequence of dream images or the dramatic structure of the dream, how can one know whether the woman's attempts to go to the "other side" of the river, however desirable, will or will not lead her into dangerous, unresolvable conflict and impasse?

The information the dream makes available gives an assessment of her situation: if she attempted an "analytic" crossing of the river, she might well become the victim of the hidden crab. Jung then attempted to discover what the unconscious kernel might be that had taken the form of the crab, and he concluded:

> The dream as it stands leaves the dreamer no alternative at present but to withdraw her foot carefully; for to go on would be fatal. She cannot yet leave the neurotic situation, because the dream gives her no positive indication of any help from the unconscious. The unconscious powers are still inauspicious and obviously expect more work and a deeper insight from the dreamer before she can really venture across. (C.W. 7, par. 165)

Everything happens as if dream elements come into contact with each other, follow one another, and are transformed according to the unconscious dynamics that they represent at the moment the dream takes place. The dramatic structure of the dream essentially sets the stage for unconscious dynamics. It thus allows the dreamer and the analyst to know the nature and the interactions of those unconscious dynamics that are at play within the time frame of the dream.

When dreams are compared with delusions and with the free associations that the patient produces while lying on the analytic couch, it is apparent that the laws that govern the concatenation of images differ according to circumstance. Images that appear within dreams, delusions, and free associations, therefore, have to be interpreted differently according to the conscious state in each of these situations.

Manifest Content—Latent Content

To discover the meaning of a dream, one has to consider the drama, which as manifest content, unfolds in the dream. Jung vigorously criticized the method of interpretation which advocates ignoring the manifest content and which, after having fragmented the dream into its elements, settles for using these elements as starting points for further associations.

> One can start from any particular point in order to free associate and invariably one will end up with a complex without ever needing a dream for that. We have made an experiment of this by using as a starting point for associations the most common of themes such as a municipal notice and even a Russian inscription. . . . Freud's central preoccupation led him to complexes and this is what he used dreams for, as we have seen in the case of the municipal notice, without ever questioning in-depth what the dreams he was using might mean. (H.D.A., p. 321, tr. RGJ)

To deny the existence of latent content is contrary to the hypothesis of the unconscious. However, the manifest content must be considered for what it contributes, which is a meaningful organization of the latent content. The task of interpretation involves allowing the flow of associations to uncover the latent contents and then bringing these latent contents back to the forms and roles they play in the manifest content.

Objective and Subjective Interpretations

The dream's latent contents originate either from within or from outside the dreamer. The dreamer's relations to external objects and to inner processes are reflected in dreams. Dreams show how the psyche receives and assimilates events and information from the external world. Dreams depict the psyche's forward and regressive movements and indicate the potential as well as the limitations of the psyche's metabolic processes. Furthermore, dreams set the stage for unconscious dynamics, their conflicts and transformations, and demonstrate the power that these dynamics have over the dreamer.

> I have therefore introduced the following terminology: I call every interpretation which equates the dream images with real objects an interpreta-

tion on the objective level. In contrast to this, is the interpretation which refers every part of the dream and all the actors in it back to the dreamer himself. This I call interpretation on the subjective level. (C.W. 7, par. 130)

A dream is a theater in which the dreamer is himself the scene, the player, the prompter, the producer, the author, the public and the critic. This simple truth forms the basis for a conception of the dream's meaning which I have called interpretation on the subjective level. (C.W. 7, par. 509)

Jung insisted that analysts can assist the dreamer toward greater self-knowledge if they take the dream figures and what these dream figures do within the dream as elements belonging to the dreamer's subjectivity. The subjective approach to dream elements makes it possible for dreamers to recognize themselves in the perceptions they have of the external world and of the object. It allows dreamers to become aware of the imagos that constitute their own psyche, which they had confused, until that point, with the external world.

Objective and subjective interpretations do justice to the complex nature of the dream. They display the dream's objective and subjective dimensions and highlight the eventual contradictions between them. The distinction between the subjective and objective planes demands that dreamers inquire whether the dream reflects an objective situation or whether it reflects a subjective attitude that distorts their perceptions of objective reality. Not infrequently, the meaning of a particular conflict will differ according to whether one takes a subjective or an objective view of the dream. A shift from one perspective to another can often free up a situation wherein the dreamer feels blocked.

The Dream's Relationship to Waking Life

The dream describes the inner situation of the dreamer, but the conscious mind denies its truth and reality, or admits it only grudgingly . . . at this point the dream comes in as an expression of an involuntary, unconscious psychic process beyond the control of the conscious mind. It shows the inner truth and reality of the patient as it really is: not as I conjecture it to be, and not as he would like it to be, but as it is. (C.W. 16, par. 304)

This is not to suggest, however, that the dream "tells the truth," in the sense that "truth" might be understood by ego-consciousness. On the contrary, the dream can lure the dreamer away from the "truth" because the unconscious factors manifest in the dream appear in response to the dreamer's conscious situation. These unconscious factors are engaged in a dialectic with consciousness and do not simply represent the unconscious.

The unconscious is the unknown at any given moment, so it is not surprising that dreams add to the conscious psychological situation of the moment all those aspects which are essential for a totally different point of view. (C.W. 8, par. 469)

Jung proposed the term "compensation" to define the dream's relationship to waking consciousness. (The concept of compensation will be explored at greater length in the next chapter.)

I call dreams compensatory because they contain ideas, feelings, and thoughts whose absence from consciousness leaves a blank which is filled with fear instead of with understanding. (C.W. 17, par. 185)

Unconscious processes are metabolized into dreams only when they are in "correlation with the present state of consciousness" (H.D.A., p. 231, tr. RGJ). It is thus necessary to refer to the dreamer's conscious state in order to properly understand the dream.

I would even assert that without knowledge of the conscious situation the dream can never be interpreted with any degree of certainty. (C.W. 16, par. 334)

In summary, Jung understood the nature of the dream in the following way:

The dream . . . furnishes the unconscious material constellated in a given conscious situation and supplies it to consciousness in a symbolical form. (C.W. 8, par. 488)

Dream and Desire

Jung discussed at length Freud's theory according to which dreams are the fulfillment of archaic desires. In reference to Freud's understanding of dreams, Jung brought up three points for consideration:

First, the dream, as seen earlier, is situated within the context of the dreamer's current life where it also plays a role.

As against Freud's view that the dream is essentially a wish fulfillment, I hold with my friend and collaborator Alphonse Maeder that the dream is a spontaneous self-portrayal, in symbolic form of the actual situation in the unconscious. (C.W. 8, par. 505)

As against Freud's view that dreams are wish fulfillments, my experience of dreams leads me to think of them as functions of compensation (*kompensatorische Funktion*). (C.W. 17, par. 185)

Second, according to Jung, the compensatory function of the dream tends to free the psyche from repetition compulsion. It will be shown later how the dream puts into action dynamics that aim to correct an imbalance within the dreamer's current attitude. Seen in the light of its compensatory function, the dream performs a creative role. Some of the dream images have a symbolic effect, while others point to the dreamer's psychological potential.

Third, the dream is co-extensive with psychic life. The dream cannot be seen from only one point of view, lest the dream lose much of what it has to offer.

> A dream, like every element in the psychic structure, is a product of the total psyche. Hence, we may expect to find in dreams everything that has ever been of significance in the life of humanity. Just as human life is not limited to this or that fundamental instinct, but builds itself up from a multiplicity of instincts, needs, desires, and physical and psychic conditions, etc., so the dream cannot be explained by this or that element in it, however beguilingly simple such an explanation may appear to be. We can be certain that it is incorrect, because no simple theory of instinct will ever be capable of grasping the human psyche, that mighty and mysterious thing, nor, consequently, the dream. In order to do anything like justice to dreams, we need an interpretive equipment that must be laboriously fitted together from all branches of the humane sciences. (C.W. 8, par. 527)

In fact, the way one talks about the nature of dreams is influenced by the way one understands desire. Freud's concept of desire as presented in Chapter 8 of the *Interpretation of Dreams* is clearly important for his dialogue with Jung. In Freud's view, desire relates to psychic mechanisms that Jung also acknowledged when he spoke about animus and anima. But Freud's definition of desire is too narrow to allow for a comprehensive understanding of dream phenomena. Freud does not account for the distinction that Lacan will later make between need and desire. Desire, according to Lacan, should not be confused with "need." Inversely, another definition currently in vogue equates libido with desire, which is too broad to account for a theory of dreams. One implication of such a view is that desire is at the origins of all psychic representations. With either approach psychoanalysis lacks a conceptual instrument necessary for understanding the specific nature of dreams.

Amplification

In addition to the effort to link dream events to the details of the dreamer's life, interpretations also have traditionally sought to establish similarities. Dream interpreters from antiquity to contemporary psychoanalysis have made use of the method called amplification, a method drawing heavily on the storehouse of cultural images.

Jung often used amplification usually to clarify the reasons for, the conditions of, and the limits to the analytic approach. When Jung amplified dream material, he stood at the juncture of two opposing perspectives.

> By nature, dream symbols are essentially individual. (H.D.A., p. 326, tr. RGJ)

> A dream, like every element in the psychic structure, is a product of the total psyche. Hence we may expect to find in dreams everything that has ever been of significance in the life of humanity. (C.W. 8, par. 527)

Contrary to the impression given by certain authors who engage in the practice of relating all of world culture to a single word or to a particular image, amplification is a precise technique. Its purpose is to achieve not a cultural or interpretative effect, but a therapeutic one. Amplification does not aim to generate meaning but to sensitize dreamers to their own inner processes.

Amplification as a method is not intended to be a means by which anything and everything can be associated to any image, or by which one analogy can slide to another. It seeks, rather, to discover the myth, the tale, the philosophical fragment, the traditional saying just as much as the work of sculpture, painting or music that will evoke emotion on the part of the dreamer and begin to open up consciousness to the dynamics manifested in the dream.

The method of amplification is sometimes misunderstood and abused. Using amplification as an excuse, some analysts tend to propose vague ideas, instead of dealing with the less attractive prospect of leading the dreamer to greater self-awareness. They prefer to profess a philosophy or an anthropology rather than do analysis. Such analysts may believe that they have already understood the dream, thereby losing the motivation to pursue further the analysand's associations to the dream imagery because they believe they have found a known schema to explain the dream imagery.

Amplification wrongly used can offer much gratification to analysands who are then pleased to see their productions raised to the status of gods, heroes, and demons. In this situation, amplification will prevent analysands from perceiving their psychic incompleteness or lack and lead them into a state of psychic inflation. Analysis can then fall sway to an imaginary, narcissistic relationship that can temporarily gratify the analysands' desire. However, under such circumstances, analysands are ultimately deprived of themselves.

On the other hand, the positive indications for the use of amplification are numerous. To begin with, amplification plays the role nowadays that myths played in former times at certain phases of the psyche's development. More and more frequently today, many people who suffer from borderline personality disorders enter analysis with the hope of having the analyst "make" them an unconscious. It is futile and destructive to confront these borderline patients with their inner lack or to make them question their motivation for coming into analysis when their psyche has not yet achieved a sufficient organization to do so. Amplification can help borderline patients validate their interior world, which otherwise often appears to them to be so fantastic and dangerous. They can be shown that their inner experience reflects an order within which others also have lived. Once they see that others share this order, borderline patients can bestow an objective value upon their own experience. They can consequently see themselves as belonging to humanity rather than feel ostracized from it.

In contrast to the legitimizing function that amplification performs for borderlines, amplification can be used to activate the unconscious of neurotics who are armored in rational defenses. Amplification is a mixture, a *Verschmelzung*, and this is precisely what some neurotics need. It offers a rare opportunity to prevent neurotics from intellectualizing analysis by sensitizing them to the poetic and archaic nature of images.

Modern men and women are out of touch with natural images, which they frequently do not take seriously. Patients often come to analysis unaware of this severe handicap. The analyst then has to take on the task of re-introducing the patient to the importance of images. Child analysts appreciate the extent to which drawings or tales help restore meaning to a disturbed symbolic function.

Finally, Jung is adamant about guarding against the danger of reducing psychic phenomena to the personal level and insists that there is another strongly influential part of the psyche that transcends the personal dimension altogether. It is important to become conscious of the psyche's "other" dimension because it stems from collective rather than personal history. This "other," or transcendent dimension of the psyche can be discerned and, in part, understood through a comparative study of collective representations.

> It must emphatically be stated that it is not just a question of cognitive contents, but of trans-subjective, largely autonomous psychic systems which on that account are only very conditionally under the control of the conscious mind and for the most part escape it altogether.

> So long as the collective unconscious and the individual's psyche are coupled together without being differentiated, no progress can be made. (C.W. 7, par. 158)

Etiology and Finality

The following texts, which characterize the Jungian approach to dreams, summarize what has been said so far:

> Dreams are not pathological but quite normal phenomena. (C.W. 17, par. 191)

> The attempt to analyze and interpret dreams is theoretically justified from a scientific standpoint. If successful, we may expect this attempt to give us scientific insight into the structure of psychic causality, quite apart from any therapeutic results that may be gained. (C.W. 16, par. 295)

> I take dreams as diagnostically valuable facts. (C.W. 16, par. 304)

But it is not sufficient to see the dream as relating solely to the past.

> An approach that uses dreams for the sole purpose of discovering the aetiological factor is biased and overlooks the main point of the dream. (C.W. 16, par. 307)

> The significance of the unconscious in the total performance of the psyche is probably just as great as that of consciousness. Should this view prove correct . . . an active orientation towards goals and purposes would not be the privilege of consciousness alone but would also be true of the unconscious, so that it too would be just as capable of taking a finally oriented lead. (C.W. 8, par. 491)

The dream serves both a diagnostic and a prospective function. It provides information that is useful in assessing the dreamer's present state. Furthermore, the dream can occasionally yield an image that sheds light upon the unknown aspects of the dreamer's life.

> [Dreams] are the undisguised (*unverfälschten*) manifestations of unconscious creative activity. (C.W. 17, par. 185)

Active Imagination

Can the unconscious be made manifest in the day world, take shape, and become a partner to the waking ego? This is what active imagination sets out to do.

It is evidently impossible to experience directly the exact nature of the unconscious. Waking fantasies, much more than dreams, distort one's experience of the unconscious. In particular, the events that take place in dreams are generally more autonomous and authentic than those encountered in conscious imaginings or even than those encountered within states of profound relaxation. Censorship and the mechanisms of defense, which lay the foundation for consciousness, confuse, divert, and cloud over the dynamic expressions of the unconscious. On the other hand, the ego is more directly involved in waking fantasies. The images produced by consciousness bear a close resemblance to narcissistic elaborations. To a greater extent than dreams, waking fantasies ask to be recognized and integrated, provided, however, that they do not deteriorate into daydreams, which can sweep the ego along and tend to dissolve any self-awareness. This is why Jung distinguished between active imagination and passive imagination.

Imagination is active if it arises and unfolds in an active field—that is, in a field where the tension between the object and the subject can be maintained. In that case, the scene that imagination displays is presented at some distance from the subject. The scene unconsciously animates the subject, while it elicits his or her reactions, much as everyday events do.

Jung began to use this method of relating to the unconscious in 1912. He wrote about the topic of active imagination for the first time in 1916 in an essay entitled "The Transcendent Function." He did not name this activity "active imagination" until 1935. However, he made allusion to it in nearly all of his works because he considered it to be as important as the interpretation of dreams.

Description

When caught by an emotion, an affect, an obsessive thought, a compulsion, or an inhibition, more often than not one reacts by using a rational interpretation: one attributes the reason for one's situation to this or that influence. It is often clear when one uses such an interpretation that one is rationalizing, thereby losing contact with the affect and abandoning oneself to the unconscious dominant that proposed the rationalization in the first place. One can ask what else one can do. Should one allow the emotion to rise to a high pitch, allow it to cry, scream, or sing, or should one freely express the drive as much as circumstances permit? By either rationalization or by hysterical discharge, tension is often dissolved; but, as a result, affect is poorly integrated. One is then left at the mercy of the drive, and the scene repeats itself later on.

Aside from getting caught within either of the two extremes of rationalization and abreaction (whether by "acting out" or by "acting in" the transference), there is another possibility: representing the affect or the drive by means of writing, or perhaps even painting, dancing, or sculpting. The affect can therefore be represented in such a way that the ego can respond as subject without having to resort to an interpretation or to any other set code. The scene unfolding within the psyche is then allowed to develop and persist. The unconscious agent takes on the form of a countryside, an animal, or a voice; it acts, expresses itself, modifies itself, while the conscious subject makes decisions, questions, and responds.

Affect presents one with an immediate vital task. It is not enough that an image simply appear. Active imagination cannot be reduced to a process that allows images to emerge or to one that brings about a catharsis. Instead, active imagination allows consciousness and the unconscious to encounter each other. The images that appear in active imagination hold claim, as much as possible, to their own autonomy. A man, a woman, an animal who may have appeared in a dream or who are called forth and visited in imagination, become for a while familiar interlocutors. Jung regularly spent time dialoguing with these figures and valued writing about them or even painting them in certain scenes, in order to maintain an objective attitude toward them.

Treating the Image like a Reality

Working with images is often seen as activity that releases psychic energies or that yields information. Yet, more often than not, the image itself is not taken seriously. Many individuals believe that the image is a trick or a mere representation. It seems so simple to fool oneself and pretend that the house did not really burn or that, indeed, it was possible to fly over the chasm. This use of the image does not respect the image's reality and betrays a need to protect oneself from it. It seduces one into playing with psychic energy without demanding that one take a stand toward it or give oneself to it. There results from this situation an unheeded dissociation that wounds one's capacity to relate to the unknown.

Becoming Involved Without a Code

Imagination presents itself as a *just-so* story and demands that the subject be entirely present to it. The consequences of the encounter between consciousness and unconscious dynamics demonstrate that unconscious dynamics are real even if they are refracted through images.

Intellectuals often engage in active imagination by seeing themselves or by hearing themselves speak. Imagination is obviously affected by their tendency to intellectualize. But in any case, each person brings who he or she is to the process; and no other norms need be followed.

Active imagination is more often indicated toward the end of analysis. It allows the patient to pursue a living relationship with the unconscious independently of the analyst's assistance. Active imagination can also be useful to those adults who feel out of step with life, by giving them the means of putting words to—and thus organizing—their interior world. Finally, those who earn a living by using empathy (such as psychotherapists) and who run a high risk of affective contagion can find a means of psychic hygiene in active imagination.

Certain critics decry active imagination and contend it is nothing more than an invitation to hysterics and a flight into the purely imaginary. This criticism is justified, but only if it refers to an imagination that is more or less passive. The criticism is not valid when it is directed at images through which the subject makes an effort to deal with concrete life situations. Under such circumstances the work with images steps out of the imaginary realm.

Chapter 3

Compensatory Dynamics

At the origin of psychoanalysis is a reflection upon the linkage of signs. This explains why Jung's first writings centered on verbal associations. It was these association studies, such as *The Psychology of Dementia Praecox*, that led him to conclude that unconscious complexes exist.

A radical change occurred in Jung's life when he broke with Freud and went his own way. From that time on Jung was preyed upon by drives, affects, and fantasies toward which he was unable to maintain an attitude of detached observer. As he reflected upon the events that befell him, he found himself without the detached perspective that his father-projection upon Freud had provided earlier. He struggled with a psychic process that he did not direct and over which he had little control. When he accepted the risk of going along with his experience, he began to adopt an epistemology different from the one he had implicitly worked from before.

Under those circumstances Jung realized that it is no longer just the intellect but the whole subject himself being called upon to make psychological observations. The subject may still be alienated, dominated by, and identified with unconscious processes, but henceforth he is called to task.

Under such conditions, the unconscious is first of all a psychic activity which, as partner *and* enemy, confronts one head-on (*Gegenwirkung*). The approach toward unconscious activity—that is, analysis—now consists of a confrontation that produces differentiation (*Auseinandersetzung*). To the extent that it modifies both the unconscious dynamics and the subject, this confrontation has a therapeutic effect.

Depth psychological thought, as Jung understands it, does not then simply reflect upon a phenomenon, but rather integrates itself into the confrontation between consciousness and the unconscious. It seeks to understand much more the modalities and the meanings of the interventions by the unconscious in consciousness than the mechanisms that govern these interventions. This is why Jung did not define the unconscious and did not construct a model of psychic apparatus. Instead, he devoted himself to the task of uncovering psychic processes.

Compensation

In the interchange with unconscious factors, the subject relies upon dreams and active imagination, within both of which unconscious factors appear in projected form. That is, these unconscious factors are separated, relatively speaking, from the behaviors with which they are ordinarily intertwined.

Given the physiological conditions under which they occur, dreams act as a constant, dynamic counterpoint to waking life. They reveal what was previously hidden to waking life and give expression to an array of other emotions. Dreams have an eye turned to waking life, which they evaluate differently than does conscious reflection.

> Even with us the collective dream has a feeling of importance about it that impels communication. It springs from a conflict of relationship and must therefore be built into our conscious relations, because it compensates these and not just some inner personal quirk. (C.W. 7, par. 277).

> We must remember the working hypothesis we have used for the interpretation of dreams: the images in dreams and spontaneous fantasies are symbols, that is, the best possible formulation for still unknown or unconscious facts, which generally compensate the content of consciousness or the conscious attitude. (C.W. 14, par. 772)

Jung's own work with dreams inspired him to make this basic statement about the unconscious: "It generally compensates the conscious content or the conscious attitude." (tr. RGJ)

In French, the term "compensation" connotes a response to a "lack." The French understanding of compensation implies giving something to someone in a way such that the person could not otherwise have it. The German meaning of "compensation" differs from the French. In German, compensation usually refers to balancing mechanisms such as those found in a clock. Compensation does not aim to fill a lack; it looks rather to correct a way of functioning. It was in this latter sense of correction that Jung used the word "compensation." He explicitly rejected the idea of "complementarity" because it would suggest a lack.

The process of psychic change relies upon the compensatory interventions of the unconscious. One can observe, in fact, that dreams most often actualize psychic elements that are opposed to those that dominate consciousness. When the latter are depicted in dreams, they are presented in such a way that the dreamer is forced to see them differently than does the waking ego. The effect is twofold. On the one hand, dreams denounce illusions and call into question what has been accepted as evident. On the other hand, during the course of analysis the psyche tends to separate itself from illusions and to resume its development to the extent that each psychic pathology or deficiency has a positive side that has remained unconscious. This positive unconscious counterpart to pathological situations emerges gradually in response to the added conscious attention that is given to the pathology.

In this way, compensation does not strive to achieve a psychic equilibrium where tensions cancel each other out, but aims at a broader functioning of the unconscious. Rather than imposing their own ideas upon compensation, analysts might best keep to listening to it and of assuring it free play.

> I always took good care to let the interpretation of each image tail off into a question whose answer was left to the free fantasy-activity of the patient. (C.W. 8, par. 400)

It appears then that dreams and, to varying degrees, other unconscious representations are a function of what the dreamer needs to hear and feel, above and beyond the repressed unconscious factors that the dream puts into dramatic form. Dreams encompass the workings of the whole psyche. This is to say that dreams express the moment and the orientation of, as well as the possibilities for, psychic development.

The interpretation of psychic phenomena must deal simultaneously with what these phenomena manifest and what they promote. This is what Jung meant when he spoke about taking finality into consideration: finality denotes a vector and thus suggests a growth process rather than a goal.

Looking at dreams from the standpoint of finality can be therapeutically fruitful. It also raises theoretical questions about the dependence of consciousness upon the unconscious, the intentionality of the psyche, the existence of an internal organization to which the compensatory function responds, as well as the conditions for a self-regulatory process within the psyche.

We will see how Jung answered these theoretical questions as we pursue our study. For the moment, however, it is necessary to examine the relationship between consciousness and the autonomous dynamics that affect it.

Conflict

The oppositional and mutually incompatible tendencies of these psychic dynamics throw one into a state of conflict, as do the incest prohibition, human limitations, and the internal tensions that force one to confront one's inner lack.

> But, just as our free will clashes with necessity in the outside world, so also it finds its limits outside the field of consciousness in the subjective inner world, where it comes into conflict with the facts of the self. (C.W. 9/2, par. 9)

> For he will infallibly run into things that thwart and "cross" him: first the thing he has no wish to be (the shadow); second, the thing he is not (the "other," the individual reality of the "You"); and third, his psychic non-ego (the collective unconscious). (C.W. 16, par. 470)

In effect, opposing psychic forces are inevitable, but must they lead to conflict? The history of psychology demonstrates that when the causes of these contradictions are understood, they can be resolved or made bearable. Many therapeutic methods aim to broaden consciousness and to facilitate its flexibility in order to allow for a stronger ego that is more readily capable of adapting to the givens of existence. Why is it so necessary, then, to experience these conflicts? Jung answered this question in several ways.

First of all, it is not everyone's fate to experience a psychological impasse where both the Yea and the Nay are equally catastrophic. Nor does this impasse appear in all psychotherapies. In many cases, conflict can be resolved by having the subject become more conscious.

At a more profound level, psychic conflict finds its source in the ego's one-sidedness and in the psyche's inner antinomies. Jung showed how contemporary history, for example, serves as a vehicle for contradictions that reverberate within individuals and toward which the monopoly structure of ego-consciousness is predisposed to react in an all-or-nothing manner. Ego-consciousness cannot avoid responding in an all-or-nothing manner without experiencing conflict.

An analogous situation exists in the case of individuals who, in seeking greater self-knowledge, come to see how the ideas that they have of themselves and of others are at odds with reality.

> For if the unconscious is not allowed to express itself through word and deed, through worry and suffering, through our consideration of its claims and resistance to them, then the earlier, divided state will return with all the incalculable consequences which disregard of the unconscious may entail. If, on the other hand, we give in to the unconscious too much, it

leads to a positive or negative inflation of the personality. Turn and twist this situation as we may, it always remains an inner and outer conflict: . . . All or us would like to escape from this admittedly uncomfortable situation, but we do so only to discover that what we left behind us was ourselves. (C.W. 16, par. 522)

Then one is left to discover that ". . . when an inner situation is not made conscious, it happens outside, as fate." (C.W. 9/2, par. 126)

Conflict is inevitable because it stems from the structural differences that exist between consciousness and the unconscious. It results from the rapprochement of consciousness with the unconscious, and it represents the first form that their coming together can take. This explains why the absence of conflict can signal an impending dissociation.

Conflict engenders fire, the fire of affects and emotions, and like every other fire it has two aspects, that of combustion and that of creating light . . . emotion is the chief source of consciousness. There is no change from darkness to light or from inertia to movement without emotion. (C.W. 9/1, par. 179)

Jung believed conflict to be at the root of the subject's progress toward self-knowledge and freedom. He conjectured, however, that there might be a state that is "free from oppositions," in which the interplay between consciousness and the unconscious might function as a kind of versatile regulator. The absence of conflict represents an ideal, but only after conflict has been overcome. This conflict-free state comes about when the subject lives with contradictions and does not back away from them.

A Third Term

We have already seen that conflict is unavoidable and plays a key role in the formation of the subject.

There is psychic conflict because the opposing terms of the conflict butt against a principle of unity: the ego. If it were not for this principle of unity, contradictory opinions, affects, and behavior would simply follow one another to be juxtaposed with each other over time. When it is caught in an impasse, such as occurs when faced with a conflict of duties within which the Yea and the Nay are equally valid, the ego experiences each one of these conflicting positions and is torn apart by their contradictory tendencies.

The ego could try to escape conflict by retreating to rationalism. It would then find refuge in collective ideas and would remain dominated by one of the poles in the conflict.

By putting up with the conflicts without splitting the poles apart from each other, the ego gradually secures its own autonomy. It keeps itself at a distance from the opposing terms and begins to accept limits.

Actually, the ego does not resolve anything: it is simply no longer dominated or influenced by a separate system of motivation. However, it can do little except contain the conflict. It must admit that the force necessary to overcome the conflict belongs to something other than itself. Thus the ego affirms itself while being at the same time defeated. The ego can do nothing but wait.

How can this situation be resolved? The solution to this problem was for Jung a foundational experience and one that oriented his practice of therapy and inspired his writings.

> Thus without noticing it, the conscious personality is pushed about like a figure on a chessboard by an invisible player. It is this player who decides the game of fate, not the conscious mind and its plans. (C.W. 7, par. 251)

> The conflict between the opposites can strain our psyche to the breaking point, if we take them seriously, or if they take us seriously. The *tertium non datur* of logic proves its worth: no solution can be seen. If all goes well, the solution, seemingly of its own accord, appears out of nature. Then and then only is it convincing. It is felt as "grace." Since the solution proceeds out of the confrontation and clash of opposites, it is usually an unfathomable mixture of conscious and unconscious factors. . . . (M.D.R., p. 335)

> Science comes to a stop at the frontiers of logic, but nature does not—she thrives on ground as yet untrodden by theory. *Venerabilis natura* does not halt at the opposites; she uses them to create, out of opposition, a new birth. (C.W. 16, par. 524)

Jung named the unexpected factor that arises from the tension of conflicting opposites the "third term." This third term is logically unpredictable and makes its appearance within the very movement that transcends the terms of the conflict.

Although he did not quite understand what he was doing at first, Jung stumbled upon this unexpected third term in 1918 when he began to draw mandalas. These images allowed him to live an intuition of wholeness which brought him out of a state of inner conflict and fragmentation, a state into which he had been caught since 1912. He discovered that psychic growth comes from the unconscious and takes place as a result of the paradoxical relationship that exists between the conscious subject—that is, the ego—and the unconscious subject, which Jung later called the Self.

The relationship between the ego and the Self is the new thing, the third term; it takes the form of a symbol, a gradient of energy, a new point of view. As a consequence of this relationship, the subject is freed from an earlier state of conflict.

Unconscious dynamics react in a compensatory manner toward consciousness. While these dynamics are at the source of psychic conflict, they also have the capacity to propose a symbol, a new orientation, or an unforeseen solution to the previous conflict, provided that the ego can tolerate the tension of opposites. In this way, these dynamics demonstrate the existence of an unconscious center of the personality.

The Detachment of Consciousness and Emptiness

The compensatory activity of the unconscious can also successfully and gradually draw the subject away from internal and external identifications which the subject had found necessary at an earlier time. Examples of internal identifications are found in beliefs, ideologies, and self-images, while instances of external identifications include persons, projects, and roles.

Dreams in particular highlight the confusions that can take place between the ego, the image, and the object. One after another, projections, incorporations, and introjections are brought to awareness by a sort of circular movement, which outlines a center within consciousness in the same way that a spinning wheel makes its axle turn, to borrow an analogy from the Chinese alchemical text, *The Secret of the Golden Flower.*

This circular process is first experienced as a sort of vertigo and then as emptiness. Jung used the expression *die Loslösung des Bewusstseins* ("the freeing of consciousness") to designate the detachment of consciousness from any object upon which a projection had been made. Detachment implies that everything is gradually called into question. Lost for the time being are the orientations, values, language, habits, contacts, and even the will to live.

> I know this effect very well from my practice; it is the therapeutic effect *par excellence,* for which I labour with my students and patients, and it consists in the dissolution of *participation mystique.* . . . When there is no consciousness of the difference between subject and object, an unconscious identity prevails. The unconscious is then projected into the object, and the object is introjected into the subject, becoming part of his psychology. (C.W. 13, par. 66)

There remains one last refuge: the myth of analysis. Consciousness can then hold up under the devastating effects of disidentification because it

is armed with the conviction that analysis leads to truth. Some individuals continue to hold to that belief in the hope of preserving a greater
peace of mind. Others discover that no definitive truth can be found in
analysis either. They realize that the unconscious speaks because there is
consciousness.

The Secret of the Golden Flower is an alchemical treatise of Taoist inspiration and speaks of the transformation of psychic energy. In contrast to
Taoist alchemy which centered on psychic energy, Western alchemy focused on the study of minerals. Jung discovered in the Taoist treatise an
attitude calling everything into question and an experience of inner
emptiness. It helped him to understand what he himself had unknow-
ingly lived through. He later became acquainted with Western medieval
alchemy texts, where he discovered in projected form the processes that
confirmed another aspect of his experience—the one that relates to the
third term about which we spoke earlier. Using alchemical texts as a
starting point, he devoted himself to the study of these processes and to
the symbolic forms they take. One must never forget that, in Jung's
view, symbols are real only if they are accompanied by deep-rooted psychic experience. Otherwise they remain caught within the realm of the
imaginary. The condition for the birth of the symbol is inner emptiness.

Chapter 4

Symbol and Feelings

Mandalas

Dreams often put forward proposals for the dreamer to consider; at other times, they call the dreamer into question. They bring into the analytic process elements of an orientation different from consciousness, and these elements evoke uncertainty and conflict. Repressed desires, new viewpoints, heretofore hidden dynamics—all serve to enlarge the conscious field by undermining current identifications.

This assault upon the dreamer's identifications can be so intense as to inflict intolerable pain. Occasionally, however, an event occurs whose origins are unknown to the subject: a symbol emerges. As stated earlier, Jung experienced what it was like for a symbol to gather power in his life when he began to paint mandalas.

During that time Jung felt that the forms that flowed through his pencils and brushes were meaningful, even though he himself did not yet know what they wanted to say. The internal upheaval he had lived through since choosing to allow the unconscious to speak gave way gradually to a feeling of wholeness and relatedness to the world.

Representation as Experience

The symbol is therefore an experience. The German language can use either of two words to distinguish between two meanings which the English term "representation" groups together: *Vorstellung* (the representation as form) and *Darstellung* (representation as activity). The symbol is a *Da(r)stellung*, "something that presents itself in the here and now."

The symbol rises "in the depths of the body" (C.W. 9/1, par. 291). It comes about as a result of a state of conflict or disorientation. "With the birth of the symbol, the regression of libido into the unconscious ceases, the blockage starts to flow again. . . ." (C.W. 6, par. 445)

Jung would then say that the symbol is a living entity. It forces itself upon the subject and mobilizes psychic energy. Jung was writing about mandalas when he stated, "These structures not only express order, they also create it" (C.W. 8, par. 870). In the case of mandalas this order consists, it seems, in having the conscious personality relate to the unconscious subject. In a general way symbolic activity is the activity of a representation that creates meaning because it joins together two separate terms. The meaningful effect brought about by the union of two separate terms has an impact on the personality, and yet this effect remains beyond rational explanation.

Relating to the Unknown

The symbol is characterized, in fact, by a certain relation to the unknown. The psychic experience the symbol creates does not come about by having one become aware of as-yet-unknown connections between already-known factors. The experience of the symbol more closely resembles the experience of rapture. A meaning—it should be repeated—grips consciousness and imposes on it, hinting at an unknown. Jung would say of this unknown that it is an *Etwas* ("a something").

> Genuine symbols point . . . to psychic contents that are not known but are merely suspected in the background. . . . (C.W. 14, par. 736)

> With regard to the terminology, it should be noted that something known is never "symbolized", but can only be expressed *allegorically* or *semiotically*. (C.W. 9/2, footnote 74)

> A view which interprets the symbolic expression as the best possible formulation of a relatively unknown thing, which for that reason cannot be more clearly or characteristically represented, is symbolic. (C.W. 6, par. 815)

The conclusion to be drawn is that not all images are symbols; far from it. Nor are symbols necessarily images. A word, an idea, a gesture can function as a symbol. "Since every scientific theory contains an hypothesis, and is therefore an anticipatory description of something still essentially unknown, it is a symbol" (C.W. 6, par. 817).

Sign and Symbol

Jung criticized Freud for reading psychic phenemona semiotically, that is to say, for interpreting psychic phenomena in a systematic way by resorting to phenomena previously known or made available through memory recall, free association, or reconstruction. This happens, for example, when one interprets psychic material from the standpoint of sexual etiology. However fruitful the sexual hypothesis may be, this kind of reading is reductive to the extent it eliminates the dimension proper to the symbol.

Nonetheless, Jung directed a similar criticism against so-called symbolic interpretations, which many believe to be "Jungian." Many would-be symbolic interpretations play with the equivocation of meanings in such a way that any connection between the symbol and real experience is lost. This way of reading the symbol does not correspond to any real experience, and simply leads the analysand into an imaginary web of meanings.

> The interpretation of the cross as a symbol of divine love is semiotic, because "divine love" describes the fact to be expressed better and more aptly than a cross, which can have many other meanings. (C.W. 6, par. 815)

> For every esoteric interpretation the symbol is dead, because esotericism has already given it (at least ostensibly) a better expression, whereupon it becomes merely a conventional sign for associations that are more completely and better known elsewhere. (C.W. 6, par. 816)

Becoming Conscious of a Symbol

The conscious subject, therefore, can attempt to deny symbolic reality by reducing the symbol to what is already known.

> Whether a thing is a symbol or not depends chiefly on the attitude of the observing consciousness. . . . (C.W. 6, par. 818)

This seems to contradict the fundamental principle according to which the symbol is a living entity only to the extent it affects the subject emotionally. "Symbols that do not work in this way on the observer are . . . extinct . . ." (C.W. 6, par. 819). In fact, the symbol is an evolving phenomenon. At the moment it emerges, the symbol actualizes and organizes a meaning that takes on all the characteristics of a fact. Individuals and groups who are affected by a symbol become believers, even if they adhere only to a theory. From this initial situation, one of two possibilities can unfold: either the symbol is allowed to exhaust itself, carrying forth less and less meaning, and eventually becoming the sign of a time past; or else in their quest for self-understanding, believers question themselves in the light of what has become for them a living symbol. Jung was very clear on this point: it behooves the subject to work with symbols and to make them conscious.

Like everything unconscious, [the symbol] signifies no more than a possibility. (C.W. 9/1, par. 280)

It all began then; the later details are only supplements and clarifications of the material that burst forth from the unconscious, and at first swamped me. It was the prima materia for a lifetime's work. (M.D.R., p. 199)

The task of going about reflecting upon symbols raises a question, however: how can one free oneself from the believer's unconscious state without destroying the symbol that promotes life? In order to answer this question, one must go back to what Jung considered to be the origin of the symbol.

All that can be ascertained at present about the symbolism of the mandala is that it portrays an autonomous psychic fact, characterized by a phenomenology which is always repeating itself and is everywhere the same. It seems to be a sort of atomic nucleus about whose innermost structure and ultimate meaning we know nothing. (C.W. 12, par. 249)

Any attempt to learn about the unconscious origins of symbols demands a close scrutiny of the forms symbols take and the conditions under which they appear. It is evident, for example, that maternal symbols do not elicit the same kind of emotional response as mandalas. To become aware of a symbol, one has to try to understand how the symbol's phenomenology presents itself and the dynamics that the phenomenology implies. It was this need to understand the phenomenological dynamics of symbols that compelled Jung to investigate mythologies.

The one and only thing that psychology can establish is the presence of pictorial symbols, whose interpretation is in no sense fixed beforehand. It can make out, with some certainty, that these symbols have the character of "wholeness" and therefore presumbly mean wholeness. (C.W. 9/2, par. 304)

The effort to understand unconscious factors cannot be a goal in and of itself. It forms part of a process that awakens consciousness to the experience of psychic reality. Hence, mandala symbols forced Jung to recognize the existence of unconscious dynamics. He sought to understand mandalas by undertaking his own self-analysis, observing his patients, comparing himself with others, and studying collective images. From these experiences and observations Jung developed the idea of the Self which, in its symbolic capacity, initiated him into a renewed relationship with the unconscious.

There can be a psychological explanation of the *filius regis* [the symbol] only when this image has sloughed off its projected form and become a purely psychic experience. (C.W. 14, par. 508)

The God of Basel

Does this attempt to understand the images of the Self not risk setting aside the need to confront the merely neurotic sources of these images? At the age of twelve Jung experienced a sort of hallucinatory fantasy, a vision that made him so anxious he was unable to admit it to himself for several days. He saw God high up in the heavens defecating on the Cathedral of Basel (M.D.R., pp. 36–8). Jung, as analyst, could have interpreted this childhood fantasy by seeing in it the work of a sadistic anal superego. However, he made no such interpretation. Instead, he drew attention to the phenomenon itself, to its emotional intensity and impact. The quality of this fantasy experience was such that Jung the child felt he had made contact with a heretofore unknown dimension of his life. It is surely valid to relate this experience to the relationship Jung had with his father; and this must be done. But it is hardly enough if one intends to respect the intentionality of the phenomenon. A semiotic reading of Jung's hallucinatory fantasy must make room for a subsequent symbolic understanding of it.

The image of the "God who shits on his church and destroys it" is for Jung something other than a semantic sign; but it is not, for all that, a metaphysical reality. On the other hand, such an image does not merely refer to an individual's desire or distress. The experience of his own superego led Jung to relate to dynamics that transcended his own individual reality.

Jung spent many years trying to understand the nature of this fantasy. His research led him to become conscious of the shadow and of the union of opposites; that is, he became aware of those unconscious organizations that are active in every human being. However, a symbol not only has this atemporal dimension. It is also present in the moment and, even then, it exhibits dynamics that transcend the subject. Is the crisis of Christian civilization not already foreshadowed, even as early as 1887, in the "God who destroys his church"? Jung discovered that the God of Basel is active throughout the psychological history of Christianity; and it is this discovery that moved him to write his *Answer to Job*.

The clinical richness of the milestones Jung observed and noted during the course of his research demonstrates the fruitfulness of his psychological hypothesis.

Numinosity

In general, when Jung took an image, an idea, or a word as a symbol, he meant to point to its emotional quality, to the way it affects the subject. He used the term "numinosity"—which is derived from the Latin word *numen*—to designate the symbol's emotional quality and force.

Numinosity, however, is wholly outside conscious volition, for it trans-ports the subject into the state of rapture, which is a state of will-less sur-render. (*Ergriffenheit*) (C.W. 8, par. 383)

Numinosity is an *Intensitätfaktor* ("intensity factor"). It corresponds to the intensity with which a representation takes over consciousness and becomes meaningful to it. It is thus an energic phenomenon. A symbol has the capacity to give and promote life because it transforms uncon-scious psychic energy into conscious experience.

Jung's observation about the emotional quality of the symbol seems simple enough. It raises questions, however, about a difficult problem: How does the analytic process take hold of psychic energy? How can analysis relate to this intensity factor?

The psychoanalytic process presupposes a dialectic relationship be-tween analyst and analysand. It demands that they discern, make con-nections, weigh, understand. This dialectic process is indebted to Freud's success in understanding that libido is symbolized through sexuality. In fact, the energy that sexuality sets into motion displaces itself, changes objects, shifts in quality, creates conflicts, and differentiates itself. This means that a Freudian approach deals with libido through the sexual forms libido takes. More recently, Lacan undertook a similar task by re-sorting to the symbolizing capacity of language and speech.

Jung understood the extent to which Freud's sexual bias tended to dis-tort the perception of psychic phenomena, and he refused to go along with it. He knew that the unconscious speaks through the emotional in-tensity of psychic phenomena, and he wondered how this emotional in-tensity could be made conscious. Can one analyze the numinosity itself of an experience or, stated differently, can psychic energy, as an inten-sity factor, enter a dialectical process?

Autonomy and Possession

Jung observed that the conscious-unconscious field is made up of a network of relations among forces of varying degrees of autonomy. The phenomena of possession, or seizure, typically relate to an energic field and correspond to the relationships psychic factors have with each other. The theory of complexes provides us with a means of understanding psy-chic life, which is made up of interactions among the more or less stable and more or less autonomous complex organizations. The energy within these psychic fields is not a "force" that belongs to the complexes but re-flects instead the quality of their relational network. From this one can lay the groundwork for studying a specific problem by reflecting upon two opposing states: autonomy and possession (*Besessenheit*).

With respect to the ego, Jung analyzed a psychic state he called the mana-personality (C.W. 7, par. 374–406). He showed how the subject who is identified with a role benefits from a surge of, and an astounding capacity to radiate energy. The subject pays for this surge and radiance of energy by causing destruction within or outside himself. For example, ideologies, slogans, fads, dictates, and theories alienate those who believe in them; yet in return, it is from them that these same believers receive energy. One thus faces a paradoxical situation: on the one hand, energy comes to the subject through the unconscious; on the other, the subject is constituted only by becoming more conscious.

The question that can be asked of analysis when it is seen from an energic standpoint can be formulated as follows: How does one preserve the energy that emanates from unconscious dynamics without falling victim to it?

Feeling: The Valuing Function

Jung considered the lures and illusions which can victimize one when he examined the fundamental phenomenon of being gripped or possessed by unconscious contents. In analyzing possession he paid particular attention to the unconscious energic relation and its emergence within consciousness in the form of psychic intensity. This intensity first emerges as an affect and later becomes a value when it is reflected upon.

> It is through the "affect" that the subject becomes involved and so comes to feel the whole weight of reality. (C.W. 9/2, par. 61)

An illusion cannot be defused, therefore, simply by being denounced and interpreted. The affect that sustains the illusion needs to be considered because it is profoundly connected to the body. If affect is not taken into account, analysis runs the risk of substituting one illusion for another while severing subjects from their roots. Words and images then become transposed into systems of meaning to which one can no longer relate; as a consequence, one's affective state regresses.

To avoid this danger, one must pay attention to the forms within which affects present themselves, which is to say one must attend to conscious values. Jung, for example, wrote the following about the interpretation of dreams:

> For dream-contents to be assimilated, it is of overriding importance that no real values of the conscious personality should be damaged, much less destroyed, otherwise there is no one left to do the assimilating. We must

see to it that the values of the conscious personality remain intact, for unconscious compensation is only effective when it co-operates with an inte-
gral consciousness. (C.W. 16, par. 338)

Must the subject be at the mercy of values that are deceptive even
though they are well-grounded? Apparently not. Jung wanted to draw attention to the specific nature of values. This is what he had in mind
when he asked the question about the *Wertschatzung*, that is, the subject's capacity to become conscious, to discriminate, and to integrate
psychic phenomena from the viewpoint of the values they impart.

As he elaborated his theory of complexes from 1907 on, Jung insisted
that complexes are charged with affect and are accompanied by libidinal
tonality and value. He continued to reflect upon the emotional value of
complexes in a short 1916 essay on "The Transcendent Function" and in
a glossary of definitions he appended to his book *Psychological Types*,
published in 1921. Jung's difficulty in grasping and formulating that
which by its very specificity eludes the categories of language is evident
in both texts. He nonetheless managed to delineate the notion of "feeling," to which he devoted an important chapter in *Aion*. Quite signifi-
cantly, this chapter is entitled "The Self."

The English word "feeling" is customarily, though perhaps incorrectly,
used to translate the German term *Gefühl*, which Jung employed. *Gefühl*
comes from the verb *fühlen*, which connotes the body, bodily sensations,
sensate discrimination in the same way it denotes affective reactions.
Gefühl is distinct from *Gemüt*, which expresses the better part of a more
or less romantic understanding of affect, which the French word *senti-
ment* and the English word *feeling* convey. The French translation that
would best correspond to the definition Jung gives to *Gefühl* would be
fonction d'évaluation, or in English, the "valuing function."

> In psychology the exact measurement of quantities is replaced by an ap-
> proximate determination of intensities, for which purpose, in strictest con-
> trast to physics, we enlist the function of *feeling* (valuation). The latter
> takes the place, in psychology, of concrete measurement in physics.
> (C.W. 8, par. 441)

What thought conceives of as a satisfaction, affect experiences as a
value. This affective experience, which is in a way the qualitative aspect
of satisfaction, results from a partially conscious and partially unconscious structure or formation. It leads to acceptance or rejection, which
is expressed in the manner of an "I like—I do not like."

Superficially, valuing appears to be a function of the ego. In fact, it is
demanded of the ego by the activity of the complexes that dominate it.

Affect is indiscriminate; the intensity of affects is not proportionate to the real importance that phenomena may have. Furthermore, the complex-orientations are mutually discordant. It is in this confusing and conflicting situation that the effort to become conscious is made, insofar as this effort enlists the valuing function. Integration is differentiation. Immature feelings are undifferentiated because they take on the characteristics of an all-or-nothing response and because they attribute values to the object that are attached to unconscious dynamics. Differentiation, says Jung, is an *Enttauschung* ("disillusionment," "disappointment"). The object that was once invested with numinosity loses its charm and fantastic quality. Differentiation takes place when subjects become conscious of the projections made upon the object, as well as when they work with the images upon which affect had once been projected. Masculine images for the woman (the animus) and feminine figures for the man (the anima) are the faces of the passion for living, for desiring, and for having bonded relationships. They express feeling variations and allow for an understanding of what deforms, twists, and refines them.

It is therefore possible to make values conscious, to question them, to confront them, and to transform the valuing process itself by respecting the specificity of the value dimension of psychic life. What is at stake in the valuing function is the ability to receive a certain type of information about the constitution of the subject and the subject's relationships with others. In fact, it is erroneous and harmful to believe that it is only through reason that one judges and decides.

> A feeling is as indisputable a reality as the existence of an idea, and can be experienced to exactly the same degree. (C.W. 16, par. 531)

The ability to appreciate reality also depends upon affectivity. But more than reason, affectivity is attuned to the information that the unconscious makes available to conscious. By its sensitivity to variations in tone and intensity, affectivity is much more rooted in the moment and receptive to what is unique in experience. The differentiation of feelings allows the subject to sort out information that is received confusedly through affect and thus to perceive the signs of what is good in the here and now.

The valuing function also plays a decisive role in analysis. If it is true that thinking and intuition disentangle the guiding threads, the bonds, and the breaks within analysis, it is by means of feelings that the analyst can appreciate the accents, silences, and nuances at work in the transference relationship. This is why the differentiation of the feeling function is critical to the analyst's formation.

The Ethical Stance

Logic can never guarantee the rightness of the decisions the feeling function makes. Feeling decisions are always logically suspect; and it is only with difficulty that they can be expressed verbally in order to be justified, for they are founded upon a personal and immediate elaboration of the irrational. They demand that one accept oneself by staying within the limits of one's own individuality. They afford the chance of becoming conscious of guiding values. Resorting to the universality of reason easily shields us from a realization of our values.

Briefly stated, the valuing function is at the root of the subject's access to personal speech. It is the valuing function that allows the subject to say "no" and "yes." By responding either negatively or affirmatively, the subject certainly has to risk becoming aggressive. But by the same token, the subject's valuing activity allows for the acknowledgment of the other's proper name. It allows for the recognition of the sign of the other's individuality and uniqueness.

> Feeling always binds one to the reality and meaning of symbolic contents, and these in turn impose binding standards of ethical behaviour from which aestheticism and intellectualism are only too ready to emancipate themselves. (C.W. 16, par. 489)

In studying symbols and feelings we came to a view that sees energy and meaning as connected to one another. We have followed Jung where he called attention to the numinosity of the symbol and to the possibility of the "dialecticization" of energy. This dialecticization of energy starts with the phenomena of autonomy and contamination. It highlights the differences in intensity that accompany each of these and further allows us to see that differences in values have impact on consciousness. Faced with the unfolding sequence of energy-affect-value, the subject can make use of the personal valuing function (*Gefühl*) as a means of integrating the energy deployed. The feeling function is sensitive to information to which reason is not receptive. It is this valuing function that grounds the "I" as it affirms itself in an ethical position.

> A content can only be integrated when its double aspect has become conscious and when it is grasped not merely intellectually but understood according to its feeling-value. (C.W. 9/2, par. 58)

Chapter 5

Images of the Other

Jung did not propose an interpretative grid to pigeonhole the manifestations of the unconscious into known categories. The categories that Jung developed in the course of his experience do not correspond to the framework of a psychic apparatus. Instead, they are of the same nature as the categories normally used to describe a personal encounter with another; they are images of the "other." Jung's approach is demanding because of the way it allows psychic phenomena to emerge and forces confrontation of the figures through which the unconscious expresses itself. The categories that result from experience correspond to the forms unconscious dynamics take as they intervene in physical and psychic life. Gradually, a grammar of the unconscious dynamics and their relations to consciousness takes shape. However, this grammar cannot be reduced to a few mechanisms. The unconscious always remains what it is—unconscious. The psyche and its rootedness in the body, in society, and in the cosmos elude the full grasp of consciousness. The major question is how one is to relate to the psyche and to its roots. The categories Jung proposed are, like the images of the "other," mediators of relationship.

These categories are constructed quite differently from concepts. Each category has three dimensions. The first dimension involves the images that appear within the individual and collective imaginary orders. A striking feature about these images, as one repeatedly encounters them, is how stable their characteristics and roles remain while they themselves take on a diversity of shapes. The second dimension refers to that aspect of the image that sets the stage for dynamics whose formation can be uncovered through anamnesis and the process of free association, both of which relate to the subject's early history, family, and milieu. The third dimension of these categories pertains to the ability to create "history," as the intrinsic character of these images manifests the nature and orientation of the dynamics at work within the subject.

Contrary to popular prejudice, dream and fantasy images comprise a vocabulary of astonishing precision. However, it is a vocabulary that is vulnerable to all kinds of abuse. The image pays for its plasticity—which allows it to signify simultaneously the nature, origins, and possibilities for integration of a psychic dynamic—by an apparent equivocation of meaning. To understand an image correctly one should pursue its analysis until only one meaning becomes possible, because only that meaning takes all of the details into account. One discovers, then, that the semantic richness of the image goes hand and hand with its precision.

Jung devoted a great deal of his work to studying unconscious dynamics and proposing guidelines for confronting them. He discerned many systems within these dynamics, which he named archetypes. Each of the archetypes corresponds to a figure of the "other," which can be found both outside of and within the subject. We will briefly examine some of these figures.

The Shadow

The uniqueness of Jung's perspective is clearly evident when one contrasts his description of the shadow with the Freudian notion of repressed contents. Jung held fast to a perspective that sees psychic phenomena as appearing to and beckoning the subject. He assumed repression but did not study it. Nor did he construct a model to explain the mechanism that produces psychic phenomena. Instead, he observed what happens to the subject and the history that subsequently unfolds.

The shadow is first of all discernible in those images that are of the same sex as the subject and that play a principal role in the subject's dreams and fantasies. "The small, brown-skinned savage who accompanied me and had actually taken the initiative in the killing was an embodiment of the primitive shadow" (M.D.R., p. 181). These personifications display character traits and ways of behaving that form the counter-part to the conscious personality. The more one-sided consciousness becomes, the more accentuated these personalities. Shadow personifications are neither complementary nor the narcissistic doubles of the conscious personality. When they are analyzed, one discovers that they embody not only repressed drives but also values that consciousness rejects. Nowadays, because the collective ideal is that of an aggressive and sexually precocious individual, the shadow takes the form of images that evoke weakness and emotionality. If it is true that the shadow personality of an old, restrained woman could be that of a flamenco dancer, then a power-oriented personality might well have as its shadow figure the image of a helpless child.

One must not conclude from these observations that the shadow is the mere opposite of consciousness. It represents, rather, what each conscious personality lacks. The shadow is for each individual what the individual might have been but has not had a chance to be. Because of this, the shadow brings to the forefront the question of identity. Who are you relative to the one you might have become? What have you done with your brother (or sister)?

This question goes beyond the issue of repression; it draws attention to what happens to all of us as a result of the choices we make. One observes, in fact, that each stand one takes generates its opposite. Thus, the forces that impel human beings to greater consciousness nourishes a sterile narcissism. For example, one who consecrates his whole life exclusively to scientific pursuits frequently leaves behind an immature feeling self. On the collective plane, the techniques that have facilitated collective life threaten to make it impossible. Industrial progress, for instance, has led to excessive pollution of our living environment. The shadow is the human being's companion and personifies for individuals and societies the consequence of their decisions.

Aside from what the personality represses while it organizes itself, and in addition to those things resulting from its choices, there exist dynamics that have not yet had the chance to become conscious; for ". . . no possibilities exist there of apperceiving [them]. That is to say, ego-consciousness cannot accept [them] for lack of understanding, and in consequence [they] remain for the most part subliminal, although, from the energy point of view, [they are] quite capable of becoming conscious" (C.W. 8, par. 366).

This observation sheds some light upon the process that "casts a shadow," a shadow that comes about through a growth of consciousness and not through the forces of repression. A considerable part of each psyche is projected upon the environment as the subject fails to attribute that part to himself. Jung called these projections "archaic identity." Once engaged in the adventure of becoming, one can observe that the psychic components once projected entirely outside appear within the individual psyche in the form of shadow figures.

This is most clearly the case when the most primitive zones of the psyche take on the form of cold-blooded animals or even of natural cataclysms. In reference to this, Jung speaks of the saurian tail that civilized peoples hide from themselves, but which they will one day rediscover.

Jung used the term "primitive" in order to designate the experience of this psychic zone.

When the different components of the psyche appear to consciousness in the forms of shadow images, they become partners to consciousness. They do so in order to allow possibility of becoming part of a mutual story. One can see the shadow react and change as one goes from a dream to the moment of becoming conscious of the dream, and from a change of behavior to another dream. The shadow nonetheless remains the Eternal Antagonist because it is born anew, taking on other forms, as a result of the subject's own development. The shadow is always "everything that the subject refuses to acknowledge about himself and yet is always thrusting itself upon him directly or indirectly . . ." (C.W. 9/1, par. 513).

In the course of this dialectic between consciousness and the shadow, the shadow can be projected upon an actual partner to whom it permits a form of homosexual attachment. It also happens that the shadow overturns the established conscious order and takes hold of consciousness in a temporary or lasting way. We are then witnesses either to contradictory behaviors or to a true upheaval of the personality, either within oneself or within another person. The second half of life is rife with these "conversions" or enantiodromias.

Becoming conscious of the shadow generally provokes conflicts that call into question habits, beliefs, emotional ties, and, more basically, the various mirrors of self-consciousness. The awareness of the shadow leads to what the alchemists called a *nigredo*, a sort of psychological crucifixion and torture. Experiencing what has been repressed or what has never been made conscious discombobulates the ego, deprives it of its bearings, and plunges it into darkness. The ego is then forced to live in a regressed state, which has characteristic features.

The experience of the shadow is for Jung the doorway to the real. The conflicts caused by the awareness of the shadow rip apart the ego's imaginary identifications. As he confronted ideologies, spiritualities, and mysticisms of all kinds, Jung kept asking himself where the shadow might lurk. He wrote, "The result of the Freudian method of elucidation is a minute elaboration of man's shadow-side unexampled in any previous age. It is the most effective antidote imaginable to all the idealistic illusions about the nature of man . . ." (C.W. 16, par. 145). "One must not turn away from what is negative, but one must experience it as completely as possible" (P.I., p. 267, tr. RGJ).

The process of self-knowledge involves "coming to terms with the Other in us . . ." (C.W. 14, par. 706).

The Persona

Jung first proposed the notion of persona in "The Relations Between the Ego and the Unconscious" (found in C.W. 7) to designate the form that the personality takes as it faces its surroundings.

> The Persona is the individual's system of adaptation to, or the manner he assumes in dealing with, the world. (C.W. 9/1, par. 221)

The persona results from the individual's gradual adaptation to the world and lasts only as long as failures in the outer world or the shadow's proddings in the inner world do not call it into question. Until it is challenged by external reality or by the shadow, consciousness can ignore just how much it had been identified with a role or an image. Then consciousness no longer has the means of knowing whether this image is suited to it or not.

> One could say, with a little exaggeration, that the persona is that which in reality one is not, but which oneself as well as others think one is. In any case the temptation to be what one seems to be is great, because the persona is usually rewarded in cash. (C.W. 9/1, par. 221)

From this point of view, the persona corresponds to Winnicott's "false self." However, it does not have this negative dimension only.

"Persona" originally referred to the mask actors wore in the theatres of antiquity. This mask made the actor's voice resound (*per-sōnāre*) while it allowed the audience to recognize the role that the actor played.

When he used the term persona, Jung meant to say that any analysis of false appearances, self-deception, and identifications to social roles must be done from the perspective of communication. Communication needs an intermediary, or medium, because there is no such thing as pure communication. Without a mask, one regresses with others into an archaic participation, or one is forced to isolate and hide oneself from others. Becoming conscious of the persona involves much more than the denunciation of what is deceitful. It is also charged with the task of inserting the subject into a social network of communication.

The mask one wears must not be suppressed. However, one has to forego identifying with it; that is, one must no longer allow a social role and language to take the place of the subject.

It is unfortunate that Jung wrote so little about the persona because his way of seeing it has the value of acknowledging the importance of the human stage or theater. This reality did not compel him to seek out misplaced "truths," but it allowed him to respond to the demands of consciousness. The persona makes it possible for the subject to be "present" while maintaining a certain "distance" from others by means of social roles. That is to say, the persona allows for communication.

The Great Mother

In his book *Symbols of Transformation*, Jung introduced to the field of analysis a new problem concerning the relationship to the mother. He thus anticipated the work of analysts who would later study the pregenital phases of childhood development. Yet Jung himself did not adopt an observer's point of view upon this topic, nor did he describe the stages of psychogenesis. Instead, he placed himself squarely within the framework of a man who had a mother as a partner at different moments in his life.

The guiding thread of Jung's thought on the mother can be found in a few pages of his 1938 essay entitled "The Psychological Aspects of the Mother Archetype." Jung evokes an image of the mother, first of all, in quasi-poetic terms:

> The positive aspect of the first type of complex, namely the overdevelopment of the maternal instinct, is identical with that well-known image of the mother which has been glorified in all ages and all tongues. This is the mother-love which is one of the most moving and unforgettable memories of our lives, the mysterious root of all growth and change; the love that means homecoming, shelter, and the long silence from which everything begins and in which everything ends. Intimately known and yet strange like Nature, loving tender and yet cruel like fate, joyous and untiring giver of life—mater dolorosa and mute implacable portal that closes upon the dead. Mother is mother-love, my experience and my secret. (C.W. 9/1, par. 172)

How can there be anything in common between this image and "that human being who was our mother, the accidental carrier of that great experience which includes herself and myself and all of mankind . . ." (C.W. 9/1, par. 172)?

In an effort to become conscious of what "mother" is, one must unravel the confusion between what is touched within oneself by the image of the mother and the human being who is its instrument.

> A sensitive person cannot in all fairness load that enormous burden of meaning, responsibility, duty, heaven and hell, on to the shoulders of one frail and fallible human being—so deserving of love, indulgence, understanding, and forgiveness—who was our mother. (C.W. 9/1, par. 172)

One must experience for oneself the maternal aspect of life.

> Nor should we hesitate for one moment to relieve the human mother of this appalling burden, for our own sakes as well as hers. It is just this mas-

sive weight of meaning that ties us to the mother and chains her to her child, to the physical and mental detriment of both. (C.W. 9/1, par. 172)

But a true and necessary separation from the mother does not merely consist in severing all bonds to her.

A mother-complex is not got rid of by blindly reducing the mother to human proportions. Besides that we run the risk of dissolving the experience "Mother" into atoms, thus destroying something supremely valuable and throwing away the golden key which a good fairy laid in our cradle. (C.W. 9/1, par. 172)

Jung was critical of any analysis that believes it has finished with the mother because it has successfully rejected the experience of her and made conscious the complex constellated in the relationship to her. Why did Jung criticize this type of analysis?

For when these fall into the unconscious the whole elemental force of the original experience is lost. What then appears in its place is fixation on the mother-imago; and when this has been sufficiently rationalized and "corrected," we are tied fast to human reason and condemned from then on to believe exclusively in what is rational. That is a virtue and an advantage on the one hand, but on the other a limitation and impoverishment, for it brings us nearer to the bleakness of doctrinairism and "enlightenment." (C.W. 9/1, par. 173)

Jung insisted upon the original power of the analysand's earliest experience with the mother. For Jung, it is this experience that is the mother; she is "my experience." The process of becoming conscious, the withdrawal of projections, the recognition of the maternal imago—these only arrive at the form of this early experience and fail to capture its substance. The power of one's experience of "mother" is then forced to project itself elsewhere and will probably do so by taking on a regressed form.

Undoing the bonds of a mother projection forces one to face up to "one's secret." The mother that can be found within oneself—whether she be marvelous or horrible, fullness or want—is no one else but oneself. To reject this "mother," or to erase her image, or to attribute her to somebody else, would only result in alienation. What else can one do? Jung suggested that the image of the mother might, in fact, be a key to the door of the unconscious.

He added: "The 'mother,' as the first incarnation of the anima archetype, personifies in fact the whole unconscious." (C.W. 5, par. 508). Not that the unconscious is mother or is in the image of the mother;

but, if one responds to the call of the mother within oneself, if one allows oneself to regress to the emotional turmoil she stirs up, one can once again have access to the unconscious. In this sense she is the door to the unconscious.

> When, therefore, Hiawatha hides himself again in the lap of nature, what he is doing is to reawaken the relationship to the mother, and to something older than the mother . . . (C.W. 5, par. 518)

> For regression, if left undisturbed, does not stop short at the "mother" but goes back beyond her to the prenatal realm of the "Eternal Feminine," to the immemorial world of archetypal possibilities where, "thronged round withe images of all creation," slumbers the "divine child," patiently awaiting his conscious realization. (C.W. 5, par. 508)

The "mother" leads the subject to renewal, that is, to a way of being that is more authentic because, through her, the subject can better relate to the unconscious. But why must one regress to the "mother"? Why does the inner child sleep and not come to us by himself or herself?

It is at this point that we enter the foreign and distant world of the unconscious matrix or womb. Jung borrowed an image from Greek alchemy to suggest what he meant: the Uroboros, the dragon that gives birth to and devours itself. The Uroboros is the image of primeval nature and of the fundamental organization of psychic energy. The very way the dragon's body develops or consumes itself when its tail fertilizes or devours its head demonstrates how psychic energy is a tension of opposites. Just like the dragon's body, energy swells or falls according to its regressive or progressive tensions. There results from this process either an expansion or, on the contrary, a suffocation and a stasis, even a degeneration into a vicious circle. Only the demands of consciousness can convert this energy into linear growth.

The image of the Uroboros corresponds to the apparently contradictory character of what one calls the Great Mother, the one who creates and destroys, who gives back life and castrates, who terrifies and protects. This Mother is immensely different from the one who, as seen from the perspective of a linear regression, was at the beginning point. She resembles much more the Good and Terrible Mother of infancy at the time splitting first occurs. But the way in which she permits the apperception of energy suggests she is the symbol that prolongs and gives power to the experience of splitting.

For Jung, in fact, the Great Mother is not a hidden power. She is a symbol, a call to the subject to experience and confront the unconscious.

Anima-Animus

Jung tells us how he became conscious of the anima. He was noting and spontaneously drawing his fantasies when a voice suggested to him that what he was producing was art. This voice troubled him, but he resisted the impulse to reflect upon it and he allowed it to speak instead.

> It had never entered my head that what I was writing had any connection with art. Then I thought, "Perhaps my unconscious is forming a personality that is not me, but which is insisting on coming through to expression." I knew for a certainty that the voice had come from a woman. I recognized it as the voice of a patient, a talented psychopath who had a strong transference to me. She had become a living figure within my mind. I was greatly intrigued by the fact that a woman should interfere with me from within. My conclusion was that she must be the "soul," in the primitive sense, and I began to speculate on the reasons why the name "anima" was given to the soul. Why was it thought of as feminine? Later I came to see that this inner feminine figure plays a typical, or archetypal, role in the unconscious of a man, and I called her the "anima." The corresponding figure in the unconscious of woman I called the "animus." (M.D.R., pp. 185-6)

One does not encounter these images only in the dialogues one has in active imagination. These images also appear within dreams and fantasies in the guise of masculine figures within the woman's psyche and as female figures within the man's. Their features do not bear any resemblance to anybody the dreamer knows but seem to belong to the dreamer's intimate world. Sometimes these figures change clothes, roles, ways of being, or age; and if one relates these transformations to the shifts that occur in the dreamer's emotional life, one discovers to what extent dream images lend a face to the unconscious factors active in waking life.

The observation of these correlations leads one to surmise that one bears traits of the opposite sex within one's own unconscious. The images of the opposite sex within the psyche are not models of the feminine or of the masculine and cannot be equated with the archetype of the woman or of the man. Jung believed that they are the psyche's predisposition to relate to the opposite sex and that they have taken shape as humanity has evolved over time.

> As we know, there is no human experience, nor would experience be possible at all, without the intervention of a subjective aptitude. What is this subjective aptitude? Ultimately it consists in an innate psychic structure which allows man to have experiences of this kind. Thus the whole nature of man presupposes woman, both physically and spiritually. (C.W. 7, par. 300)

> The anima can be defined as the image or archetype or deposit of all the experiences of man with woman. (C.W. 13, par. 58)

Jung turned the usual understanding of the anima upside down when he asserted that the feminine element within the man's psyche does not appear by having the man internalize the mother's image, any more than the woman's animus comes about by having the woman internalize the father's image. One's parents are, rather, the first external actualization of this innate predisposition.

> Nor is she (the anima) a substitute figure for the mother. On the contrary, there is every likelihood that the numinous qualities which make the mother-imago so dangerously powerful derive from the collective archetype of the anima, which is incarnated anew in every male child. (C.W. 9/2, par. 26)

> Every mother and every beloved is forced to become the carrier and embodiment of this omnipresent and ageless image, which corresponds to the deepest reality in a man. (C.W. 9/2, par. 24)

We will see, when we study the notion of the archetype in the second part of the present book, how Jung related the concept of "image" to that of "structure." For the moment, let us say that the anima and the animus project themselves in images that appear not only in dreams, literature, or mythology, but also in the emotional behavior and life of the subject. They organize everything that relate to the sexual identity of the subject, in particular, oral and anal eroticism, fantasies of castration, and Oedipal relationships. The anima and the animus are not, therefore, merely the virtual or projected images of the opposite sex. They become, as a result of experience, autonomous complexes that place considerable pressure upon the ego complex. To the extent that these complexes remain unconscious, their activity is principally negative.

> In its primary "unconscious" form the animus is a compound of spontaneous, unpremeditated opinions which exercise a powerful influence on the woman's emotional life, while the anima is similarly compounded of feelings which thereafter influence or distort the man's understanding ("she had turned his head"). (C.W. 16, par. 521)

The anima and the animus are not symmetrical. Each produces its own effect. The unconscious anima possesses a man by plunging him into a mood, while an unconscious animus possesses a woman by having her blurt out unreflected opinions (C.W. 7, par. 331). Jung explored mostly the anima's influence and power:

> The unconscious anima is a creature without relationships, an autoerotic being whose aim is to take total possession of the individual. When this

happens to a man he becomes strangely womanish in the worst sense, with a moody and uncontrolled disposition which, in time, has a deleterious effect even on the reliable functions—e.g., his intellect . . . (C.W. 16, par. 504)

It belongs to him, this perilous image of Woman; she stands for the loyalty which in the interests of life he must sometimes forgo; she is the much needed compensation for the risks, struggles, sacrifices that all end in disappointment; she is the solace for all the bitterness of life. And, at the same time, she is the great illusionist, the seductress, who draws him into life with her Maya—and not only into life's reasonable and useful aspects, but into its frightful paradoxes and ambivalences where good and evil, success and ruin, hope and despair, counterbalance one another. Because she is his greatest danger she demands from a man his greatest, and if he has it in him she will receive it. (C.W. 9/2, par. 24)

These complexes, which are particularly active in couples' relationships, ignite passions just as often as they instigate quarrels.

Whereas the cloud of "animosity" surrounding the man is composed chiefly of sentimentality and resentment, in woman it expresses itself in the form of opinionated views, interpretations, insinuations, and misconstructions, which all have the purpose (sometimes attained) of severing the relation between two human beings. (C.W. 9/2, par. 32)

No man can converse with an animus for five minutes without becoming the victim of his own anima. (C.W. 9/2, par. 29)

When animus and anima meet, the animus draws his sword of power and the anima ejects her poison of illusion and seduction. The outcome need not always be negative, since the two are equally likely to fall in love (a special instance of love at first sight). (C.W. 9/2, par. 30)

Very often the relationship runs its course heedless of its human performers, who afterwards do not know what happened to them. (C.W. 9/2, par. 31)

One does not free oneself so easily from the grip of either the animus or the anima.

The effect of anima and animus on the ego is in principle the same. This effect is extremely difficult to eliminate because, in the first place, it is uncommon and immediately fills the ego-personality with an unshakable feeling of rightness and righteousness. In the second place, the cause of the effect is projected and appears to lie in objects and objective situations. Consciousness is fascinated by it, held captive, as if hypnotized. Very often the ego experiences a vague feeling of moral defeat and then behaves all the more defensively, defiantly, and self-righteously, thus setting up a vicious circle which only increases its feeling of inferiority. (C.W. 9/2, par. 34)

The ability to put such a possession in perspective is acquired only gradually as subjects differentiate the anima and the animus from themselves and from parental imagos. This differentiation most often begins to take place when the shadow starts to call the subject into question.

> It is only when one has a knowledge of the shadow that one meets up with the anima. The same condition holds for the animus: So long as the shadow remains unrecognized, women are possessed by the animus. (E., p. 33, tr. RGJ)

The anima and the animus are transformed and their influence becomes positive and contributes to the maturity of the psyche to the extent that the ego becomes conscious of them and frees itself from the grip of their possession.

> His anima wants to reconcile and unite; her animus tries to discern and discriminate. (C.W. 16, par. 522)

> Just as the anima becomes, through integration, the Eros of consciousness, so the animus becomes a Logos; and in the same way that the anima gives relationship and relatedness to a man's consciousness, the animus gives to woman's consciousness a capacity for reflection, deliberation, and self-knowledge. (C.W. 9/2, par. 33)

In our present society, a feeling connection to others is still for men, just as self-affirmation and speech continue to be for women, the attributes of the unconscious sex, the contrasexual. The animus and the anima are most often projected beyond the everyday world and upon the prestigious powers of the Eternal Feminine, the Hero, and the Wise Old Man or the Wise Old Woman of the mythological realm. A man can integrate his capacity for emotional bonding, and a woman her capacity for speech, if each substitutes a relationship to the anima or to the animus for a possession by them. Sexual identity is not acquired merely by the concrete exercise of sexuality. It also demands an internal confrontation with the contrasexual aspects of the personality.

Sexual identity occurs in particular as one becomes aware of desire. Even though he does not use the term "desire," Jung recognized the images of desire in the anima and animus. The anima, whom he speaks about in *Memories, Dreams, Reflections*, did not inspire him to create a written opus. She offered him an ability to savor life. The object and the satisfaction that the anima and the animus provide are but the means to an intensity and a zest that impart a passion for rigor, heroism, or pleasure, and a fondness for loving love. The animus seeks the security and the power it can find in logic and truth, whereas the anima makes an idea a successful one by giving it an aesthetic touch. In this way, both the animus and the anima draw the personality they dominate into a

secondary auto-eroticism from which the personality derives content-
ment by means of the actual representations of pleasure. The personality
that is caught within this secondary auto-eroticism becomes prisoner to a
subjectivity that is without object or subject.

Inversely, when one is able to recognize the anima and the animus in
such a way that they no longer exert an unconscious influence over the
ego, their effect is transformed. The animus and the anima can then play
the role of mediator to the unconscious. It is in their capacity for mediation that Jung ultimately defined the animus and the anima. For him,
the mediation between the unconscious and consciousness is sexual in
nature; and this mediation is achieved through the unconscious sex.

Jung summarized his ideas about the evolution of the relationship
between the anima images and consciousness in the following way.

> Thus the insinuations of the anima, the mouthpiece of the unconscious,
> can utterly destroy a man. In the final analysis the decisive factor is always
> consciousness, which can understand the manifestations of the uncon-
> scious and take up a position toward them.

> But the anima has a positive aspect as well. It is she who communicates
> the images of the unconscious to the conscious mind, and that is what I
> chiefly valued her for. (M.D.R., p. 187)

> For decades I always turned to the anima when I felt that my emotional
> behavior was disturbed, and that something had been constellated in the
> unconscious. I would then ask the anima, "Now what are you up to? What
> do you see? I should like to know." After some resistance she regularly
> produced an image. As soon as the image was there, the unrest or the
> sense of oppression vanished. The whole energy of these emotions was
> transformed into interest in and curiosity about the image. I would speak
> with the anima about the images she communicated to me, for I had to try
> to understand them as best I could . . . (M.D.R., pp. 187–8)

The Ego and the Self

Jung's clinical experience with psychotics led him to inquire very early
on into the psychological constitution of the subject. In his everyday
work at the Burgholzli Hospital, he witnessed how consciousness was
shattered when it fell victim to autonomous processes. The fundamental
problem that occupied Jung concerned the unity and organization of the
psyche. From 1907 on, starting with his book *The Psychology of Dementia
Praecox*, Jung raised the issue of the nature of the ego, a question about
which most psychoanalysts of his day cared little. He proposed a theory
which sees the psyche as a cluster of complexes that are more or less
independent and opposed to one another. According to Jung's formula-

tion, the ego itself is a complex, in fact the complex that usually constitutes the central axis of consciousness.

> But inasmuch as the ego is only the centre of my field of consciousness, it is not identical with the totality of my psyche, being merely one complex among other complexes. (C.W. 6, p. 425)

> . . . the individual ego . . . in its banality [is] that continuous centre of consciousness whose presence has made itself felt since the days of childhood. (C.W. 8, par. 182)

> We understand the ego as the complex factor to which all conscious contents are related. It forms, as it were, the centre of the field of consciousness; and, in so far as this comprises the empirical personality, the ego is the subject of all personal acts of consciousness. (C.W. 9/2, par. 1)

The ego is not only a subject; it is also itself a content of consciousness. First, like any other complex, it is composed of a group of representations and affects that are combined on the basis of heredity and learning.

> The ego consists of its memories and affects. . . . (H.D.A., p. 347, tr. RGJ)

> The ego, as a specific content of consciousness, is not a simple or elementary factor but a complex one which, as such, cannot be described exhaustively. Experience shows that it rests on two seemingly different bases: the somatic and the psychic. (C.W. 9/2, par. 3)

Jung states that, from the somatic point of view, "the ego is the psychological expression of the firmly associated combination of all body sensations" (C.W. 3, par. 83).

From the psyche's point of view, the ego "seems to arise in the first place from the collision between the somatic factor and the environment, and, once established as a subject, it goes on developing from further collisions with the outer world and the inner" (C.W. 9/2, par. 6).

Like all other complexes, and in spite of the fact that it is the center of consciousness, the ego is partially unconscious. This means that the ego projects itself in imaginary formations such as the Persona (for Jung), or the Ideal Ego and the Ego-Ideal (for Freud).

> Set against this overpowering force is the fragile unity of the ego, which has come into being in the course of millennia only with the aid of countless protective measures. (M.D.R., p. 346)

To the extent that the other complexes—such as the parental complexes, the shadow, the anima and the animus—are autonomous, they take on the characteristics of "secondary subjects" (C.W. 8, par. 366) and occasionally function in the role of the ego, unless they completely engulf the ego for long stretches of time. Jung will say that when complexes occasionally function in the role of the ego, they act as "dominants of consciousness" (C.W. 8, par. 403) and that when they completely engulf the ego, they possess or inflate the personality.

Some people are astonished that Jung did not speak of narcissism. In fact, he analyzed narcissistic phenomena using a different epistemology.

The concept of narcissism actually results from an external point of view of the phenomena in question. Unlike the concept that bears his name, however, Narcissus directly experienced an insatiable quest for the self and acute anguish in the face of everything that threatened his self-image. Jung took up Narcissus' subjective experience and discovered the *Ichhaftigkeit* ("ego attachment") within which the subject is caught. This internal force seeks the constitution of an ego complex around which it wants all of psychic life to revolve. Before the ego differentiates itself by relating to the unconscious, it is in a state of *Ichsucht* ("ego addiction") (C.W. 14, par. 364), a turning of consciousness upon itself. The danger then is that the image of the world and the image of the ego risk becoming confused with one another.

Ichhaftigkeit (C.W. 11, par. 554) might well dominate the individual psyche if its own one-sidedness did not give birth to the shadow, which becomes in turn an independent complex opposed to the ego. The ascendancy of the shadow (of which the return of the repressed is but one aspect) overturns the organization of the ego. Jung analyzed the transformation process that then begins. Rather than focusing upon narcissism, he studied the conflicts, sacrifices, and mutations that mark the successive moments of the subject's formation.

Jung insisted upon the fact that becoming conscious puts the ego in jeopardy. A 1941 text reflects what he himself had lived through thirty years earlier:

> The integration of the contents split off in the parental imagos has an activating effect on the unconscious, for these imagos are charged with all the energy they originally possessed in childhood, thanks to which they continued to exercise a fateful influence even on the adult. Isolation in pure ego-consciousness has the paradoxical consequence that there now appear in dreams and fantasies impersonal, collective contents which are the very material from which certain schizophrenic psychoses are constructed. (C.W. 16, par. 218)

Even while it endures such an ordeal, the ego cannot escape from an inflation, be it a negative or positive one. While relating to its own solitude and to the psychic elements it integrates, the ego either allows itself to become possessed by an upsurge of psychic energy or defends itself from this energy by identifying with its own conscious boundaries. Is there no way to avoid these two false solutions?

> But at this point a healthful, compensatory operation comes into play which each time seems to me like a miracle. Struggling against that dangerous trend towards disintegration, there arises out of this same collective unconscious a counteraction, characterized by symbols which point unmistakably to a process of centring. This process creates nothing less than a new centre of personality, which the symbols show from the first to be superordinatae to the ego and which later proves its superiority empirically. The centre cannot therefore be classed with the ego, but must be accorded a higher value. Nor can we continue to give it the name of "ego," for which reason I have called it the "self." To experience and realize this self is the ultimate aim of Indian yoga and in considering the psychology of the self we would do well to have recourse to the treasures of Indian wisdom. In India, as with us, the experience of the self has nothing to do with intellectualism; it is a vital happening which brings about a fundamental transformation of personality. I have called the process that leads to this experience the "process of individuation." (C.W. 16, par. 219)

Thus by becoming conscious and by withdrawing projections, the ego is led into a state of either inflation or deflation. Neither of these states is resolved unless an unconscious center of the personality to which the ego can relate is brought to life.

> The centring process (Zentrierung) is, in my experience, the never-to-be-surpassed climax of the whole development, and is characterized as such by the fact that it brings with it the greatest possible therapeutic effect. (C.W. 8, par. 401)

What is such a center? For his first inkling, Jung turned to the mandalas he painted while he experienced this center. Mandalas "portray the self as a concentric structure, often in the form of a squaring of the circle. . . . The structure is invariably felt as the representation of a central state or of a centre of personality essentially different from the ego. It is of numinous nature . . ." (C.W. 14, par. 776)

> It can make out, with some certainty, that these symbols have the character of "wholeness" and therefore presumably mean wholeness. As a rule they are "uniting" symbols, representing the conjunction of a single or double pair of opposites. . . . (C.W. 9/2, par. 304)

Mandalas thus suggest that this unconscious dynamic has the following characteristics: center, totality, principle of unity, conjunction of opposites, structural quaternity. Yet Jung refrained from generalizing from these hypotheses and did not weave them into a theory until he read the Chinese alchemical text *The Secret of the Golden Flower*, which Richard Wilhem brought to his attention in 1928.

Even though this text does not speak of the Self, it describes the phases one goes through following a radical loss of identification with objects and representations. It also evokes the fire which subsequently flows "within the cavern of emptiness." Jung discovered that the experience described within this text came close to his own; and he went on to elaborate the idea of the Self, a term he borrowed from the *Rig-Veda*.

> I knew that in finding the mandala as an expression of the self I had attained what was for me the ultimate. Perhaps someone else knows more, but not I. (M.D.R., p. 197)

From this time on Jung devoted the better part of his research to understanding the Self and the individuation process. In the spring of 1934, he overcame his resistance and plunged into the reading of Western alchemical texts. He wrote *Psychology and Alchemy* (1944), *Psychology of the Transference* (1946), *Mysterium Coniunctionis* (1955–56), and many other studies. Later, he returned to the study of Christian Gnostic texts. He sought to clarify, one in the light of the other, his patient's dreams, his clinical observations, and collective images. He wrote about Christian themes in *Aion* (1951), *The Answer to Job* (1952), and several other studies, among which is *Transformation Symbolism of the Mass* (1954).

It is impossible here to develop the Jungian theory of the Self. I would like, however, to suggest an outline of key ideas that relate to Jung's understanding of that concept.

During the first period of his studies on the Self, Jung especially emphasized the fact that the Self is first projected upon mythological and theological figures before it becomes known. Is not the idea of the One God who is the center of the world the projection upon the cosmos of what exists in the psyche? Has the process that frees an individual from the imaginary and gives him or her psychological birth not been attributed to the figures of the Anthropos in several evolved cultures? Does the conscious realization of an unconscious impulse that gives meaning to life not actualize what was announced by the coming of Christ and the incarnation?

Influenced as he was by alchemy, Jung focused less upon images and more upon processes. The conjunction of opposites, with all that it implies of separation and differentiation, provides the schema with which one can understand the activity of the Self. Jung summarized this activity using three concepts: (1) becoming follows upon a compensatory movement; (2) wholeness consists of the relationship of consciousness with the unconscious; (3) psychic organization evolves according to the law of differentiation.

When referring to the concept of wholeness, which Jung used frequently, one must recall that the English word *totality* obscures the original German meaning. Jung rarely used *die Totalität* but almost always *die Ganzheit (ganz, ganzwerden)*. Now the root prefix *ganz* does not signify "total" but "whole." It would be better to translate *Ganzheit* by the English "wholeness." Far from aiming to become, possess or experience everything, the *Ganzheit* is correlative to the experiences of dissociation and fragmentation. Jung specified that *Ganzheit* is not a *Volkommenheit*, not "a total achievement, perfection." To individuals who feel the presence of two beings within themselves, *Ganzheit* appears as a possible unity. It is in the sense of a possible unity that the experience of the Self resolves the dissociation of consciousness from the unconscious and allows the subject to be whole.

Jung's experience of the Self came as a sort of illumination. He perceived within himself the meaning of his existence and of analytic therapy. This is why he was first of all inclined to depict the Self as encompassing two extreme theses. According to the first thesis, the Self is the true center of the personality from which the ego, by its values and goals, is alienated. Thus the ego must sacrifice its goals and values if it is to submit to the orientation of the Self. This sacrifice is brought about by the recognition of the shadow and has the characteristics of what some will later call a symbolic castration. Sacrifice differs from symbolic castration, however, because sacrifice does not culminate in the mere acceptance of human limitations and death but leads to a living relationship with the unconscious subject.

The abandonments, losses, and mournings that the personality has to experience as it becomes more conscious make the sacrifice of the ego somewhat analogous to the traditional Oriental teachings about the death of the ego. After attempting a few hesitant formulas, Jung clearly distinguished these Oriental traditions from analytical experience.

> Naturally there can be no question of a total extinction of the ego, for then the focus of consciousness would be destroyed, and the result would be complete unconsciousness. (C.W. 9/2, par. 79)

What is at stake in the analytic process is not the death of the ego but the sacrifice of *Ichhaftigkeit* ("ego attachment"). Not only does the ego not disappear, but the conflicts that it goes through release it from imaginary states and allow it to come to its own reality.

Having discovered the existence of the Self, Jung strongly emphasized its importance. Only gradually did he pay attention to the role of the ego, eventually insisting that its function is as irreplaceable as that of the Self. Jung showed in *Answer to Job* how ego-consciousness is the only psychic agent that responds to the internal contradictions of unconscious powers. Ego-consciousness is both the condition for the unity of these contradictions and the principle that forces them to be inscribed in history.

The ego is the only subject responsible for making choices and for becoming ethically involved. It alone has to bear the responsibility for the decisions it makes.

> The ego is endowed with a power, with a creative force that is humanity's latest achievement, which we call the will. (H.D.A., p. 90, tr. RGJ)

Jung recognized in *Mysterium Coniunctionis* that the ego is the absolute condition for the objective existence of the world.

The second thesis Jung proposed about the Self is that the ego and the Self are interdependent, even though the opposition between them is an opposition between illusion and truth, respectively. He denounced both the rationalistic danger of not recognizing the Self and the mystical danger of absorbing the ego within the Self.

> However, accentuation of the ego personality and the world of consciousness may easily assume such proportions that the figures of the unconscious are psychologized and the self consequently becomes assimilated to the ego. (C.W. 9/2, par. 47)

> For the self has a functional meaning only when it can act compensatorily to ego-consciousness. If the ego is dissolved in identification with the self, it gives rise to a sort of nebulous superman with a puffed-up ego and a deflated self. (C.W. 8, par. 430)

The human subject is actualized by means of an inner polarity—that is, by means of the paradoxical coordination of the conscious and unconscious centers. But these two centers are not of the same order: the Self is not simply a "deep" ego.

> The difference between knowledge of the ego and knowledge of the self could hardly be formulated more trenchantly than in this distinction between "quis" and "quid." (C.W. 9/2, par. 252)

Chapter 6

Transference

The images we form of the "other" are in fact parts of ourselves. From the beginning of our existence, our surroundings permeated our very substance. If there is to be any hope of clearing up the consequent ambiguity between what comes from oneself and what comes from the surroundings, this ambiguity needs to be transferred into the pristine space of an entirely new psychic relationship. This is what analysis sets out to do.

"Unsticking" Projections

Following the initial stage of anamnesis, one's first experience in analysis is undoubtedly to experience the affects and reactions toward the analyst that one believes were originally inspired by one's own parents. That one attributes these affects and reactions to the analyst leads to the suspicion that one's subjectivity is confused with the object. This also leads one to think that the traits one attributes to the analyst, in fact, belong to oneself. Thus transference displaces upon a third person those psychic contents that took shape when the subject first began to relate to the environment and with which they are still identified.

This is a general phenomenon, and it devolved upon psychoanalysis to bring it to awareness.

> The transference itself is a perfectly natural phenomenon which does not by any means happen only in the consulting-room—it can be seen everywhere. . . . (C.W. 16, par. 420)

Analytic transference differs, however, from those transferences that occur in everyday life. In contrast to everyday transferences, the analytic transference takes place in a delimited field where the analyst does not respond to projections but stops them, frames them, and presents them to the analysand's consciousness.

In making these interpretations, the analyst must of course use the feeling function. We have already seen how interpretation comes about through a process of valuing. No objective, abstract knowledge can take the place of a personal feeling for the analytic relationship and process. It is useless to pretend that the analyst's valuation does not affect the outcome of certain phases of the analysis.

The feeling involvement of analysts in the analytic process is not dictated by a moral code. Therapists know that a feeling involvement in the analytic process forms part of their destiny as therapists and that it results from the responsibility they bear toward the patient. Common sense observation points out that one treats oneself the way one treats others. The kind of psychological mediation analysts provide is, in fact, unique. Analysts can observe within their own reactions to their analysands' transferences a reflection of their own attitude towards themselves.

Similarly, the analysand has to contend with the analyst's anima or animus without regard to the technique the analyst uses. Interpretations, gestures, silences, and physical layout of the office speak of this secret part of the analyst's psyche. The risk of a mutual involvement of the analyst and the analysand would not be possible if it were not for the eventual positive participation of the unconscious. This is true even if this mutual involvement does not produce anything emotionally unusual. Certain dreams comment upon, correct, complete, and reorient the analysis. The analyst's participation owes much to the existence of unconscious processes that are capable of repairing, reorganizing, and promoting psychological growth.

Becoming a Couple

We started with the idea of a need for a new psychological space, but we have come to discover the possible fruitfulness of a confusing situation. The two belong to each other, for the transference is at once a space of utmost neutrality allowing for projection and also a process that is set into motion by the existence of that space—that is, by the relationship between analyst and analysand.

> Medical treatment of the transference gives the patient a priceless opportunity to withdraw his projections, to make good his losses, and to integrate his personality. (C.W. 16, par. 420)

Jung believed the transference to be essential to analysis. In 1913, he wrote the following:

Thanks to his personal feeling, Freud was able to discover wherein lay the therapeutic effect of psychoanalysis. (C.W. 4, par. 427)

Here Jung is speaking of the transference. Again, in 1929, he wrote:

It is one of Freud's outstanding achievements to have explained the nature of this tie, or at least the biological aspects of it, and thus to have facilitated an important advance in psychological knowledge. (C.W. 16, par. 140)

Finally, in his last work, Jung added the following remarks:

The main problem of medical psychotherapy is the *transference*. In this matter Freud and I were in complete agreement. (M.D.R., p. 212)

The reference to Freud is amazingly emphatic and suggests that Jung saw his understanding of the transference to be a natural extension of Freud's. He adopted as his own, in fact, the classic rules that govern the analyst's behavior; and he conducted analytic work in such a way as to facilitate the use of concepts and guidelines proposed by authors who claim to be Freud's followers.

For Jung, as well as for these Freudian authors, the role of the analyst is seen to be that of a mirror for, and partner to the analysand. The analytic role leads us to the awareness that the unconscious enfolds us and, in a way, clothes the world. The psyche is an interlocutor who participates in a dialogue within which the as-yet-unknown parts of ourselves are projected.

Jung ended up clearly affirming that the psychotherapeutic relationship is founded upon psychic contagion.

The patient, by bringing an activated unconscious content to bear upon the doctor, constellates the corresponding unconscious material in him, owing to the inductive effect which always emanates from projections in greater or lesser degree. (C.W. 16, par. 364)

Psychic contagion refers then to countertransference. True to his approach to the unconscious, Jung refused in every way to repress this confused zone; on the contrary, he endeavored to let it speak (*geschehenlassen*). This zone is the living point of an encounter. "They [spontaneous archetypal events] are immemorially strange and unknown . . ." (C.W. 16, par. 501).

However broad it may be, a state of mutual unconsciousness is the source and essence of the analytic relationship. To respect this fact, Jung eschewed all methodological preconceptions and made this fundamental observation:

A person is a psychic system which, when it affects another person, enters into reciprocal reaction with another psychic system. This [is] perhaps the most modern formulation of the psychotherapeutic relation between physician and patient. . . . (C.W. 16, par. 1)

He pushed this observation to its final conclusion:

If I wish to treat another individual psychologically at all, I must for better or worse give up all pretensions to superior knowledge, all authority and desire to influence. I must perforce adopt a dialectical procedure consisting in a comparison of our mutual findings. . . . In this way his system is geared to mine and acts upon it; my reaction is the only thing with which I as an individual can legitimately confront my patient. (C.W. 16, par. 2)

Such sentences evoke fear. The analyst is portrayed as being quite without resources, and the risks for confusion are quite great. The defenses that patients and therapists alike hope to preserve are lost once the reality of this relationship is accepted. Analysts are called upon, from the depths of their own being, to be totally present to the analytic situation.

The crucial thing is no longer the medical diploma, but the human quality. (C.W. 16, par. 74)

"Ars requirit totum hominem," we read in an old treatise. This is in the highest degree true of psychotherapeutic work. (C.W. 16, par. 400)

In their capacity as therapists, analysts are called upon to confront the unconscious.

We must suppose as a matter of course that the doctor is the better able to make the constellated contents conscious, otherwise it would only lead to mutual imprisonment in the same state of unconsciousness. (C.W. 16, par. 365)

It is up to analysts to create the conditions for a confrontation between consciousness and the unconscious, a confrontation made possible by having analysts attend (betrachten) to the analytic process in such a way as to frame and objectify whatever would otherwise slip away or be taken up only to be judged. Analysts set up tensions in the analysand's conscious field and join the analysand in an exchange of energy, much like two systems that are connected to each other. Analysts may, at difficult moments, find themselves alone having to fill the role of the ego and having to maintain the tension generated by conflicting opposites.

Toward the end of this work, analysis terminates fairly naturally. Analysis has made possible the expansion of consciousness, the strengthening of the ego, and a certain regulation of drives. It has helped the patient adapt to others and to himself or herself.

If, however, the projection is broken, the connection—whether it be negative (hate) or positive (love)—may collapse for the time being so that nothing seems to be left but the politeness of a professional tête-à-tête. (C.W. 16, par. 447)

In fact, analysis does not always evolve this way. It sometimes gets stuck in the analysand's ill-defined demands or breaks down for no apparent reasons. Analysts discover then that they are no longer dealing with the transference of projections but with the transference of lacks. They are confronted by their analysands' urgent demand for reparation; and everything happens as if analysands and analysts believed that the analytic relationship were capable of meeting these demands, at least to a certain extent.

It also happens that the transference develops into a demand for intimacy with the analyst. This demand is as impossible to analyze reductively as it is to satisfy. Analysts know that they could call the analysands back to the "reality" of their contract, or that they could interpret the transference in terms of infantile projections. But analysts may, in such situations, sense the dangers of resorting to rationality. Something indeterminate yet life-promoting might be wounded if such reductive interventions are made. The analysands' demand for intimacy seems to express, albeit in maladapted ways, the necessity of accomplishing an as-yet-unknown task. As it throws the ordinary course of analysis into confusion, this demand gives the impression that it touches upon the essential core of the transference.

Within a Mutual Unconscious

Those situations within which unmanageable transferences occur are fraught with difficulty. To clarify the transference phenomenon, the nature of the analytic relationship needs to be examined more deeply.

Two dimensions of the transference are closely related to each other: the original transference process, implying transformation, underlies the second process, the withdrawal of projections. A number of difficulties arise, however, when we are unable to distinguish clearly between these two dimensions. This can take place when the analyst and the analysand unconsciously collude with each other in seeing the demand inherent in the transference as anything other than a repetition of childhood desires. Conversely, they may substitute for analysis a grand project of transformation, which remains caught within the imaginary. But anyone who is aware of the two dimensions of the transference is in a better position to perceive the orientation of the analytic relationship, which we may call its actual intentionality. The informed analyst knows, then, whether the analysand is engaged in a growth of consciousness, requiring of the analyst above all neutrality, distance, and possibly frustration—or whether the time has come for a more profound psychic upheaval, which a dialectical relationship demands (cf. C.W. 16, par. 1).

It was important for Jung to note the difference between these two dimensions of the transference and to draw attention to the reality and the nature of the transference as a process, because no one before him had analyzed it in quite that way. A transference becomes a neurosis when it is not allowed to unfold into a story.

Reflecting the difference between the "transference-work," which deals with projections, and the "transference-process," which relates to transformation, Jung wrote about a patient in the following way:

> The personal relationship to me seems to have ceased: the picture shows an impersonal natural process. (C.W. 9/1, par. 531)

What might be going on in this situation? A mutual state of unconsciousness, which binds the analyst and the analysand to each other, forms a couple. This analytic couple is not exogamous, as are the couples that constitute the basic unit of society; it is, rather, endogamous.

Exogamy regulates the conscious relationship of the analysand and the analyst. But kinship libido, however strongly repressed it may be today, permeates their unconscious relationship. In accordance with a model that is unique to it and that was known within ancient civilizations as the *Hieros gamos* or the triad of marriage-prostitution-sacredness, endogamy organizes the analyst and the analysand's unconscious relationship to each other. The *Hieros gamos* was a counterpart to legal marriage, as if the power that unites couples needed to have two forms, legal and psychological.

While giving the appearance of utmost neutrality, the analytic couple brings together people who are secretly colluding with each other: the analyst and the analysand share a similar taste for the psyche, its problems, and its resources. What a "family"! Indeed, what an incestuous relationship!

Jung clearly acknowledged that the analytic relationship is based upon incest. Unlike those who glimpsed this incestuous reality but remained bent on denying it in the name of the incest prohibition, Jung accepted it just as it is and endeavored to understand its meaning and implications.

He saw incest as an original state, a moment within which the difference between woman and man is still unstable and in danger of being lost in the union that attracts the sexes to each other. It is vitally important to prevent this regression; any subsequent maturation depends upon the capacity to prohibit this union. But, inversely, the propensity in analysis toward incest draws its power from its goal: to bring consciousness back to its unconscious sources.

By the time he wrote about the transference, Jung had already confronted for quite a while the paradox of incest. He knew that the unconscious dynamics are not merely the after-effects of a psychic formation, but that they are also at its source. In Jung's view, incest symbolyzes, by way of union with relatives, the problematic conditions of the subject's conjunction with past and present origins. How can one get in touch again with these original processes without falling into the unconscious —that is to say, without becoming possessed by it? This is, indeed, a risk.

What happens when the incestuous wish is prevented from being concretely lived out but when the reality and the feeling value of what animates it are nevertheless recognized?

The Process

Jung found in the alchemical text *Rosarium Philosophorum* a series of woodcut prints that illustrate the history of an incestuous couple. He saw these woodcuts as depicting less an allegory than a projection of what unfolds between the analyst's unconscious and that of the analysand. He commented on these prints in 1946 in *The Psychology of the Transference*.

The first image (see fig. 1) in the series of woodcuts portrays a basin filled with water and a fountain from which water also flows. What is at stake is that neither dryness nor flooding prevail but that spring water flow and be contained.

Now couples parade through (see fig. 2): sun and moon, king and queen, brother and sister, each pair forming a couple by having one partner hold the other's left hand. Analyst and the analysand, who for that matter can be of the same sex, are of course nowhere depicted. What is shown, however, is the crisscrossing of their unconscious relationship. We can say that analysands encounter the analyst's mediating function, which is feminine in men and masculine in women. Analysands, for their part, enter into the analyst's mediating function through their own sexual duality. Thus multiple relationships between analysts and analysands, which clinical experience teaches us to recognize, become possible. To a large extent, these relationships direct the analysand's choice of analyst, because the intensity of the transference and the possibilities of treating it vary according to whether the analyst is or is not of the same sex as the analysand.

Jung did not adapt his commentary to reflect the many variations that

Figure 1. The Mercurial Fountain. (This appears as Figure 1 in the *Rosarium Philosophorum* [Jung, *The Psychology of the Transference*, 1946, p. 205].)

Figure 2. King and Queen. (This appears as Figure 2 in the *Rosarium Philosophorum* [Jung, *The Psychology of the Transference*, 1946, p. 213].)

occur in the clinical setting. He presented the structure of the process and left it up to the reader to discern the specific forms it takes in the therapeutic context.

In the third and fourth pictures (see figs. 3 and 4) the king and queen have abandoned the garments of their conventional relations. They are naked and, somewhat humorously, drenched in the fountain. This suggests that, in the initial stages of analysis, analysands gradually reveal their shadow side to their analysts, who keep theirs veiled. But it happens eventually that analysts make a mistake: an error, a forgetful moment, a lapse, they stumble—a small thing perhaps, yet their shadow appears. This is a moment of truth. Will the analyst readjust by throwing the question back upon the analysand? How will the analysand be able to stand exposure to someone who is no longer merely a technician or, on the other hand, a god? Many analysands stop analysis here. Some return to their former attitudes as if nothing had happened, while others

Figure 3. The Naked Truth. (This appears as Figure 3 in the *Rosarium Philosophorum* [Jung, *The Psychology of the Transference*, 1946, p. 237].)

FIGURE 4. **Immersion in the Bath.** (This appears as Figure 4 in the *Rosarium Philosophorum* [Jung, *The Psychology of the Transference*, 1946, p. 243].)

criticize the analyst for imperfection and for having abandoned them. Others feel freed of a projection that once paralyzed them: analysts are no longer "they who know." These analysands thus take along with them as they leave the analytical context their new-found capacity to relate more authentically.

For the benefit of those whom the unconscious does not leave in peace and who need to go further, the next image in this series (see fig. 5) depicts intercourse. Certain versions of these prints show the two protagonists as having wings in order to dispel all concretistic fantasies and to emphasize the psychic character of the union taking place. These protagonists have agreed to join each other in their adventure toward greater consciousness, albeit by playing different roles and by adhering to their own truth.

Eros animates the relationship, but prohibition kills it. In fact, death appears in the sixth print (see fig. 6). This means that what might have appeared to gratify analysands tears them apart just that much more.

Understanding, sincerity, the absence of any recourse to technique or protection then become so many more open and vulnerable sores. The conflict is just that much more profound, the lack just that much more torturous, as a total realization seems to lie within easy reach.

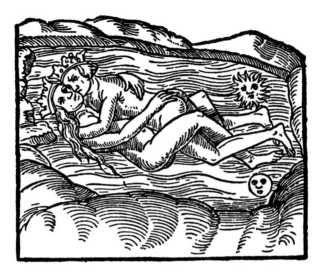

Figure 5. The Conjunction. (This appears as Figure 5 in
the *Rosarium Philosophorum* [Jung, *The Psychology of the
Transference*, 1946, p. 249].)

The long period of depression and purification (see figs. 7 and 8) has
begun. The seventh print shows a soul flying away: depression, like
death, is a loss of soul. The protagonists have become a single body with
two heads; and, like an empty shell, they lie in a tomb. Analysts know

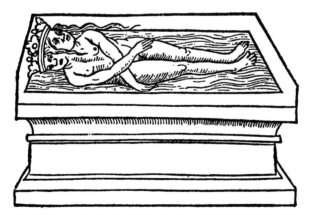

Figure 6. Death. (This appears as Figure 6 in the *Rosarium
Philosophorum* [Jung, *The Psychology of the Transference*,
1946, p. 259].)

Figure 7. The Ascent of the Soul. (This appears as Figure 7 in the *Rosarium Philosophorum* [Jung, *The Psychology of the Transference*, 1946, p. 269].)

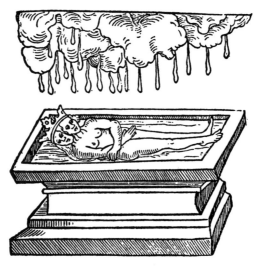

Figure. 8. Purification. (This appears as Figure 8 in the *Rosarium Philosophorum* [Jung, *The Psychology of the Transference*, 1946, p. 275].)

to what extent they themselves participate during this period in their analysands' pain, emptiness, and loss of meaning. It is as if analysts were so much of one body with their analysands that they are, at times, unable to recoup their strength at the end of a session. The analytic process is a tomb within which anguish and the desire for death are set free. Often analysands discharge their anguish and desire for death against their analyst, whom they accuse of being responsible for this morbid state.

Jung noted the importance of making sure that analysands have some guidelines to help them understand what they are experiencing. Without any apperceptive concepts—that is, without any categories with which to receive the events—integration is impossible. The initiatory passage through death was, in former times, always accompanied by a discourse that revealed to the initiates the meaning of what they were experiencing. Such teaching is necessary, but it is dangerous. It offers, in a much more subtle way than any sexual acting-out could, the opportunity to re-establish an intellectual or spiritual fusion; and it can thereby be an invitation to regress.

In the ninth figure (see fig. 9) the tomb is open, and within it lies an androgynous being toward whom a small human silhouette descends. Breath returns.

The mythology of the androgyne projects a simple psychic reality upon a dubious image. This mythology signifies that the analysand now finds "within" what had previously been asked of a partner of the opposite sex in the "outside" world. Incest has blossomed and born fruit. The relation to the unconscious is mediated by way of a relationship with the inner partner. The animus for the woman and the anima for the man combine the Same and the Other. They mediate the radical differences between the inner and the outer.

Transference has used up the energy constellated within it. In this situation, Jung said the analysand's relationship with the unconscious can continue through the use of active imagination. The analysand also begins, at this time, to perceive the uniqueness of each human being. And his or her relations to others becomes truly sexual.

The Birth of the Symbolic Capacity

The last image in the series (see fig. 10) depicts a new birth. The androgyne, wearing two crowns, rises up victorious upon a quarter moon, while the tree of life grows next to him. This is probably the one illustration that is least congruent with the analytic process. The alchemists in their time were unable to project what we are dealing with today.

During the death phase, the conflict opposing the demands of con-

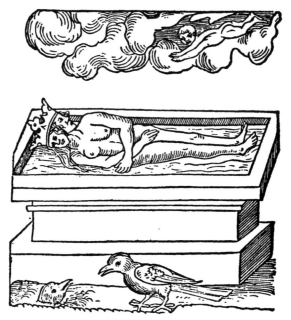

Figure 9. The Return of the Soul. (This appears as Figure 9 in the *Rosarium Philosophorum* [Jung, *The Psychology of the Transference*, 1946, p. 285].)

Figure 10. The New Birth. (This appears as Figure 10 in the *Rosarium Philosophorum* [Jung, *The Psychology of the Transference*, 1946, p. 307].)

sciousness to those of the unconscious gradually separates the ego from the anima and the animus. At the same time, it throws the ego into a state where it no longer knows anything or controls the situation. The ego can only hold on and wonder what the outcome will be: Can unconscious dynamics, which up till now supported the process, bring the process to term?

Once life returns, it brings a new element to the process. The dynamism that sustained the process is now capable of being symbolized. This process appears to consciousness in forms that Jung saw as belonging to the phenomenology of the Self. The ego can now relate to this process through the images of the Self that appear to consciousness. The subject, which is constituted by the relationship between the ego and the Self, has at its disposal a new symbolic function that allows it to apprehend an object from either a conscious or an unconscious center. It is in the symbolic function arising from the conjunction of opposites that Jung saw the principle of humanization at work.

You

The Jungian view of human evolution is that it is erotic. The relation to the unconscious, the relationship between the ego and the non-ego, the conjunction of opposites—all of these are at play in men's and women's relations to each other.

> Looked at in this light, the bond established by the transference—however hard to bear and however incomprehensible it may seem—is vitally important not only for the individual but also for society . . . it is accomplished in a sphere but lately visited by the numen, where the whole weight of mankind's problems has settled. (C.W. 16, par. 449)

Discovering the conjunction of opposites and the existence of the Self, Jung then applied himself to determining the nature of the Self and to representing the pathways that lead to it. He wrote little about object relations, but he denounced the illusion that would advocate separating the analysand's confrontation with the unconscious from relationships with other human beings. He asserted that whoever isolates himself or herself cannot attain wholeness:

> But the conscious achievement of inner unity clings to human relationships as to an indispensable condition, for without the conscious acknowledgment and acceptance of our fellowship with those around us there can be no synthesis of personality. (C.W. 16, par. 444)

> The unrelated human being lacks wholeness, for he can achieve wholeness only through the soul, and the soul cannot exist without its other side, which is always found in a "You." (C.W. 16, par. 454)

PART TWO

Reflections on the Relations Between Consciousness and the Unconscious

Chapter 1

Epistemology

The first part of this book drew the broad outline of an analytical approach to the unconscious. This approach is based on the fact that psychic phenomena most often appear without the subject willing or understanding them. The subject has no choice, then, but to objectify them, to understand the personal reactions to them, and to take a stand regarding them. Once these conditions are met, changes occur. One can acquire a practical understanding of these phenomena by observing them. This practical understanding includes a familiarity with reference points, an ability to deal with psychic phenomena, and a knowledge of the confrontation with them.

Is this practical understanding sufficient, however? The analytic approach to the unconscious must also be studied; and this inquiry should address two issues: (1) whether this approach to the unconscious can be justified, and (2) how this approach can add to an understanding of the phenomena with which it deals. These two questions are the focus of the second part of this book.

In the effort to answer the first question, a Jungian approach must formulate its epistemological presuppositions and its therapeutic intent. Jung's epistemological presuppositions are investigated in this chapter. The purpose of his therapeutic approach will be covered in the last.

Operational Value of a Concept

As he carried out his work, Jung took pains to make explicit the epistemology that underlies it. Jung was not always understood and his contemporaries were misled by his ability to hold apparently contradictory points of view simultaneously.

Jung understood psychological concepts to be themselves psychic phenomena. Once cannot deal with these concepts only in relation to their content. The meaning they impart cannot be separated from the role they play. It is first of all this role that Jung examined:

> The moment one forms an idea of a thing and successfully catches one of its aspects, one invariably succumbs to the illusion of having caught the whole. . . . This self deception certainly promotes peace of mind; the unknown is named, the far has been brought near, so that one can lay one's finger on it. One has taken possession of it, and it has become an inalienable piece of property, like a slain creature of the wild that can no longer run away. (C.W. 8, par. 356)

Jung did not think that concepts grasp and represent objects; rather, he saw them as tools that are used to shape the real. He wrote the following in a 1913 essay, "The Theory of Psychoanalysis":

> I have taken as my guiding principle William James' pragmatic rule: "You must bring out of each word its practical cash-value, set it at work within the stream of your experience. It appears less as a solution, then, than as a program for more work, and more particularly as an indication of the ways in which existing realities may be changed. Theories must become instruments, not answers to enigmas in which we can rest." (C.W. 4, par. 86)

The concepts that Jung thereafter formulated do not reduce their objects to a univocal transcription. The meaning of Jung's concepts include both a reference to time and a relation to the "other."

The animus concept signifies, for example, (1) the *position* from which one discerns the phenomena that will subsequently be defined as animus, (2) the *dynamics* that arise from desire and that organize, at one and the same time, a woman's way of thinking and her self-affirmation, (3) the *representations* and *behaviors* that are characteristic of the masculine symbolic register within a given society, (4) a mediating *function* to the unconscious, (5) the *transformations* that take place in all of these elements taken as a whole. Concerning this latter point, the nature of the animus varies according to whether it is confused with the parental imagos, or is just beginning to be differentiated from them though it still dominates consciousness, or is separate from the ego to which it is in relation.

Speaking about the animus affords a means by which specific psychic phenomena can be brought to the conscious field. The concept of the animus is capable of doing this to the extent that it is not an abstraction but a concept relating to an experience.

An Experiment or an Experience?

The experience we are discussing cannot meet the standards that positivism has set for itself. It is not an *experiment* in the sense normally understood as research conducted by a detached observer acting upon something observed. It is rather an *Erfahrung*, a lived experience in which the observed and the observer are one and the same person.

Jung defined "empirical" to mean the lived interaction between the subject and the events that happen to the subject. We have already shown how this lived experience becomes conscious according to a process defined by the three verbs *geschehenlassen* (to allow to happen), *betrachten* (to consider), and *sich auseinandersetzen* (to confront oneself with). Little can be said of Jung's thought without making reference to this process. It is the experience of this process that forms the basis for an understanding of Jung's approach to the psyche.

> Nobody can really understand these things unless he has experienced them himself. (C.W. 7, par. 340)

> I can, therefore, produce nothing convincing, nothing that would convince the reader as it convinces the man whose deepest experience it is. (C.W. 7, par. 364)

These quotations are logical extensions of the principle Jung proposed when he was president of the International Psychoanalytical Association in 1911: *No one can be an analyst unless he or she has first undergone a personal analysis.*

The reason for this prerequisite is that in the study of psychology there is no detached or disinterested observer. Jung is adamant on this point and holds to a rigorous phenomenalist position.

> Every psychic process is an image and an "imagining," otherwise no consciousness could exist and the occurrence would lack phenomenality. Imagination itself is a psychic process, for which reason it is completely irrelevant whether the enlightenment be called "real" or "imaginary." (C.W. 11, par. 889)

It is in this way that Jung defined the field of endopsychic perception, beyond which no one can have the point of view of the psyche.

Jung was not a phenomenologist, however, because he was not a philosopher. He was first and foremost a therapist. For him, the phenomenon is essentially what works: "What is real is what acts." An action does not take place in the indeterminate. It occurs in a conscious field and in relation to someone. Experience presumes a subject and contributes to forming that subject who is doing the experiencing.

> Only that which acts upon me do I recognize as real and actual. But that which has no effect upon me might as well not exist. (C.W. 11, par. 757)

Some of these phenomena appear to vary in degrees of autonomy and strangeness. They seem to arise from unknown structures and centers of activity. Thus, within the empirical realm, an intention can appear that transcends and has a point of reference beyond consciousness of the moment.

What can we know of what lies beyond consciousness? That which lies beyond consciousness is in itself inaccessible, yet we can analyze the myriad signs of its activity. Psychic experience is not merely an individual matter; it also has a collective dimension. Whereas different subjects experience differently the interplay of psychic dynamics, the forms these dynamics take are seen to be repetitive. These repetitive forms can be found within the rituals, the beliefs, the lifestyles, and the past of humanity. They remain meaningful patterns still active today in different individuals. If one keeps this observation in mind, one can manage to distinguish the personal from the collective. Jung believed that any particular psychic phenomenon points beyond itself to an unknown that is manifested in collective forms.

The development of Jung's thought went through two phases, each of which made use of a different epistemology. In the first phase, Jung confronted the unconscious and succeeded in formulating the conditions of that confrontation, its categories and reference points. In the second phase, Jung compared collective material gathered from human history with the elements gleaned from individual experience. It was during this second period that Jung formulated his hypothesis concerning conscious and unconscious organizations and the evolution of the relationship between them.

Contrary to the claims of some commentators, the second phase of the development of Jung's thought is not affiliated with any hermeneutics. His comparative method is part and parcel of his personal understanding of psychic phenomena. The comparative method is a growth-promoting activity. As the subject experiences it, the collective itself is charged with emotions, power, meaning, and meaninglessness. It acts. The comparative method makes no attempt to indulge cultural interests; rather, it has the subject confront collective representations and the unconscious that speaks through them.

As such, a theory has no definite value. "As I saw it, a scientific truth was a hypothesis which might be adequate for the moment but was not to be preserved as an article of faith for all time" (M.D.R., p. 151). A scientific truth is not, however, merely a fiction. In the final analysis, it either promotes life or brings on death. One does not think without paying a price. In Jung's view, a theory is a symbol.

Thus the theory of the collective unconscious, which is to be examined in subsequent chapters, is at once the putting into form of one experience and the beginning of another. Jung's theory acknowledges that psychic phenomena have a kind of consistent autonomy, so a theory presents a new polarity in endopsychic perception. The collective unconscious, which appears first of all as an object through the forms that represent it, becomes a subject and perceives consciousness as its object. Is it not the subject who comes to the unconscious rather than the other way around? Jung does not hesitate to consider both points of view in several texts. For example, . . . if we take them [conflicts between opposites] seriously, or if they take us seriously . . . (M.D.R., p. 335).

The decision to adopt one point of view over another is not only an intellectual exercise. Affectivity finds itself caught between two opposing inclinations, one that is empirical, the other transcendent. It is these two orientations together that characterize the experience we are trying to account for. Jung's idea of wholeness refers to the possibility of experiencing psychic phenomena as a function of either a conscious or an unconscious center.

What does this all mean for the subject?

The Two Mirrors

> Of the essence of things, of absolute being, we know nothing. But we experience various effects; from "outside" by way of the senses, from "inside" by way of fantasy. (C.W. 7, par. 355)

Consciousness has two mirrors at its disposal. Dreams, fantasies, attitudes, and the unconscious dimension of the body all react to what appears true according to criteria defined by the concrete world. Conversely, other people, society, and the needs of the body each judge those fantasies, desires, dreams, and thoughts. Psychoanalysis attempts to make sense of so-called internal representations by resorting to drive theory, object relations, and the demands of the reality principle. The reality principle, however, is not absolute; and psychoanalysis would fall into a rationalist trap if it endeavored to "deduce the inner world from the outer" (C.W. 9/1, par. 187).

Jung refused to judge the unconscious according to the standards of the outer world. He held the view that the external and internal worlds, as opposites, are differentiated in successive phases; and he showed that the individual is constituted by means of a two-fold confrontation. Far from treating concrete reality as an ultimate reference point, Jung demonstrated how the subjective and objective worlds, both external and internal, reciprocally shape each other.

Each of these systems has its own laws and dynamics. Each one reacts to, sorts out, judges, and analyzes what comes from the other. If the reality of these two mirrors is accepted, no unilateral identification with one point of view over another is allowable. The ability to hold together the two contrary points of view is a measure of the subject's psychological health.

> Failure to adapt to this inner world is a negligence entailing just as serious consequences as ignorance and ineptitude in the outer world. (C.W. 7, par. 204)

This dual mirror of inner and outer worlds is, nonetheless, more than an adaptation to two opposing sets of demands. It is a dual source of information that acts upon the subject and brings about transformation.

The psychic entity we call the subject is first of all the ego, faced as it is initially with poorly differentiated outer and inner worlds. Jung explained this lack of differentiation by stating that "it is the natural and given thing for unconscious contents to be projected" (C.W. 8, par. 507).

> Indeed, one could even define [the ego] as a relatively constant personification of the unconscious itself, or as the Schopenhauerian mirror in which the unconscious becomes aware of its own face. All the worlds that have ever existed before man were physically there. But they were a nameless happening, not a definite actuality, for there did not yet exist that minimal concentration of the psychic factor, which was also present, to speak the work that outweighed the whole of Creation; that is the world, and this is I! That was the first morning of the world . . . the ego, the son of the darkness knowingly sundered subject and object, and thus precipitated the world and itself into definite existence, giving it and itself a voice and a name. (C.W. 14, par. 129)

The story unfolds well beyond these first steps. The differentiation of the inner world from the outer, which results from increased self-awareness, places the ego more and more into a state of conflict. This continues to happen until there emerges another point of view, which acts as another center, through which the subject is finally constituted.

> The self is a "mirror". . . . (C.W. 11, par. 427)

Another evaluation, other projects, another vision of the world comes to us from that center, the Self. It is one of Jung's major contributions to psychoanalysis that he recognized the existence of this unconscious center.

> That is to say, although the psyche can never know anything *beyond* the psyche . . . it is still possible for two strangers to meet within the sphere of the psychic. They will never know themselves as they are, but only as they appear to one another. (C.W. 17, par. 161)

History

Each pole of psychic life elaborates, reconsiders, and sends back what it receives from the other. Each affirmation must be tested by its opposite.

> To the critical intelligence, nothing is left of *absolute* reality. (C.W. 7, par. 354)

> Everything is flux. (M.D.R., p. 351)

However, the subject is a stumbling block. When one happens upon the subject, the question of integration is raised. The subject forms ties, within itself and within its relationships with others, to what would otherwise go on in endless cycles. It is by means of the subject—because the subject is a body and will die—that movement becomes history.

> Truth is not eternal, it is a programme to be fulfilled. The more "eternal" a truth is the more lifeless it is and worthless; it says nothing more to us because it is self-evident. (C.W. 6, par. 87)

Is this to say, for that matter, that psychology becomes history? Curiously enough, no. One could say that, for Jung, everything was historical. No discourse on history, however, is found in Jung's works. He attributed a determinative importance to the "living psychic process," without in any way proposing a psychogenetic theory. This is because the analytic perspective he adopted does not take an external point of view of the psyche. If Jung appreciated the psyche's links to the past and its orientations to the future, it was always in relation to the continuous unfolding of history.

When he insisted upon the need to return to beginnings, Jung specified that he was referring to the need to return to the imago. Even the prenatal state refers to the imago and not to an actual past condition. In a parallel fashion, the concept of finality refers to a purpose in the present and not to an aim that is directed toward a pre-established goal.

Jung was so strongly accustomed to apprehending psychic phenomena in the present that he was led to think that " . . . the forms of psychic orderedness are acts of creation in time" (C.W. 8, par. 965). Within the analytic framework, the analyst has to rediscover each analysand's time frame and help the analysand grow at his or her own pace, without emphasizing any one dimension at the expense of another.

The Energic Point of View

Jung called libido physical energy in order to differentiate it from other types of energy. But, in defining libido, he refused to attach to it any quality that would in any way confine it to a particular sphere of symbol-ization, such as sexuality.

> Libido is intended simply as a name for the energy which manifests itself in the life-process and is perceived subjectively as conation and desire. (C.W. 4, par. 282)

Form and energy are reciprocal. We therefore cannot define energy by pointing to one of its forms, even if this form is a privileged one.

It is currently thought that an idea, an image, or a behavior takes on a form as a result of pre-existing factors and that this form unleashes activ-ity. Energy would, according to this view, be the quality of the form. This view clearly reflects a mechanistic schema. The analytic approach to the unconscious presents an alternate model. Every psychic fact re-flects a moment of a context and history to which it belongs. Form and role are one and the same for a given psychic fact. That is, the role re-flects the development the system's energy undergoes. The mandala, for example, is just as much an image of an activity as it is the activity of an image. One can distinguish an image from its activity only by the way in which one considers all of the phenomena in question.

> Libido, therefore, is nothing but an abbreviated expression for the "energic standpoint." (C.W. 8, par. 56)

We have seen in Chapter 4 of Part 1 how the reciprocity of form and energy finds its support and justification in the dialecticization specific to energy. The reciprocity of form and energy is the psychoanalytic coun-terpart to the work with signifiers.

When talking of energy it is difficult to prevent imagination from picturing it as something: a flow, an *élan*, a force. Nevertheless energy is known not to be a potential but a gradient. Jung held firmly to this view. He illustrated his stand by formulating the law of compensation he used in the interpretation of dreams. For him, psychic phenomena come about as a function of one another. Their intensity and impact depend on the polarities within which they are caught. Tensions can arise in any of the following areas: between the subject and the internal and external mirrors; among the intentionalities that contradict each other in the present; between subjects and even between different moments in time. All of these situations demonstrate that the psyche is characterized by multiple differences of potential.

Jung did not hypostatize libido into a motor-force of evolution, in con-trast to the vitalist fantasy. Libido, if left to itself, would probably be sta-tionary or spasmodic. The observing ego with its questioning attitude and its inexorable needs are necessary if differentiation is to occur at all.

"We know as little about what underlies [libido] as we know about what the psyche is *per se*" (C.W. 5, par. 195). Whether or not one takes the energic point of view when approaching the psyche is not inconsequential. The choice, which determines the course of analysis, depends upon the ego.

Attention will focus upon shifts, transformations, and processes —keeping track of disjunctions, separations, assimilations, conflicts, and shadows. Relationships become apparent and, along with them, the network of tensions within which whatever happens is inscribed and interpreted. The origins of an appreciable portion of Jungian categories and of the vocabulary in which these categories appear can thus be discerned if one attends to such psychic material.

Life-Value

> Man woke up in a world he did not understand, and that is why he tries to interpret it. (C.W. 9/1, par. 65)

To a man who does not have any reason to take one stand rather than another, ". . . scientific theories are merely suggestions as to how things might be observed (*betrachten*)" (C.W. 4, par. 241). In those situations where one remains content to be an observer, one makes use of criteria that are outside oneself. But what can one do with a psychology within which one must function oneself?

> What is decisive . . . is uniquely and only the life-value that the patient discovered and the fact that the patient found a solution within this value. (G.W. XIV/2, par. 365, tr. RGJ)

> Only the course of the individual's life can decide this, i.e., his individual experience. There are no abstract criteria. (C.W. 11, n. 37)

Jung never forgot that he was a therapist. The ultimate criterion by which he judged therapeutic approaches lay in the "life-value," in whatever way a person may experience this. In this way, Jung integrated his theory into the healing arts. In fact, theory in his view is a symbol, which suggests and even imposes an attitude toward life. And this view of theory led him to wonder how theory affects the person who adheres to it.

Do we not then end up in a radical subjectivism, which leaves all individuals to their own illusion provided that it suits them? The answer to that question has to be no, since an affirmative answer would imply the End of History, as Hegel pointed out. There can be no answer to this question as long as humankind is still evolving.

Again, Jung held firmly to two different views: on the one hand, that the only criterion to be followed is each person's own life and on the other that the person's life is not limited to his or her conscious opinions and moods. The individual's life is caught by and plays a role within a set of dynamics which assault, criticize, and pursue it through external facts and the unconscious.

Chapter 2

Archetypes

The idea of the "archetype" has been the source of much misunderstanding among Jung's followers as well as among his critics. The danger lies in not going beyond a single formulation of the archetype and in not following through a gradual and difficult theoretical elaboration to its logical end.

Inherited Systems

In 1910 Jung had already abandoned the idea that the psyche begins to take shape only after birth.

> Man "possesses" many things which he has never acquired but has inherited from his ancestors. He is not born as a tabula rasa, he is nearly born unconscious. But he brings with him systems that are organized and ready to function in a specifically human way, and these he owes to millions of years of human development. . . . man brings with him at birth the ground-plan of his nature, and not only of his individual nature but of his collective nature. These inherited systems correspond to the human situations that had existed since primeval times; youth and old age, birth and death, sons and daughters, fathers and mothers, mating, and so on. Only the individual conscious experiences these things for the first time, but not the bodily system and the unconscious. (C.W. 4, par. 728)

He does not yet use the term "archetype," but the basic idea is already there: The psyche consists of unconscious predispositions that make possible an organized human existence. Archetypes, which have slowly evolved through the course of history, are *a priori* conditions to actual experience.

Original Images (*Urbilder*)

In order to know and analyze these unconscious predispositions, Jung took the path opened up before him by images.

As he listened to his patients' spontaneous imaginings and dreams, Jung was surprised to encounter the same images, situations, and scenes in the dreams of many different patients, but also in fairy tales, myths, and stories indigenous to diverse cultures.

> Over the whole of this psychic realm there reign certain motifs, certain typical figures which we can follow far back into history, and even into prehistory. . . . They seem to me to be built into the very structure of man's unconscious, for in no other way can I explain why it is that they occur universally and in identical form. . . . (C.W. 16, par. 254)

As early as 1911-1912 when he wrote the *Symbols of Transformation*, Jung compared different hero myths to the fantasies and the life of a woman patient (Miss Miller) whose case Flournoy had studied. This comparative study clarified for Jung the unconscious processes that lead to symbolic sacrifice and incest. At that time, Jung called the schema common to a set of collective and individual representations an original or primordial image (*Urbild*).

He stated more precisely, and rather vehemently later on, that his goal in formulating this theory of the primordial image was therapeutic and not hermeneutic.

> It is inevitable that the mythologem and its content will also be drawn into the limelight. This is not to say that the purpose of the investigation is to interpret the mythologem. But, precisely in this connection, a widespread prejudice reigns that the psychology of unconscious processes is a sort of philosophy designed to explain mythologems. (C.W. 7, par. 436)

In fact, Jung was particularly sensitive to images. He observed that his patients' psychic difficulties disappeared, or at least were attenuated, once patients began to understand and sense the images underlying their difficulties. For many years, Jung was little inclined to pursue his theoretical reflections further.

When he advanced the concept of archetype for the first time in 1919 in "Instinct and the Unconscious" (found in C.W. 8), he chose a term that connoted far more the idea of *model* than of *process*. He borrowed the term from St. Augustine for whom this word signified ". . . a *typos* [imprint], a definite grouping of archaic character containing, in form as well as in meaning, mythological motifs" (C.W. 18, par. 80). The French dictionary *Petit Robert* defines the word *archetype* to mean the following: "A primordial type or idea—an original that serves as a model, an exemplar." The word refers to a fixed, normative concept and does not easily lend itself to the meaning Jung would later give to it.

The Image Clears the Way (*Bahnung*)

Jung observed, in fact, that the image not only makes an imprint but also directs activity as well. Dreams and fantasies organize human behavior, even when the subject is not conscious of them, in the same way that myths in primitive times suggested possible answers to life's principal problems.

The image is not then a flat representation like a poster. It is a "functional form"; and " . . . the term 'image' is intended to express not only the form of the activity taking place, but the typical situation in which the activity is released" (C.W. 9/1, par. 152).

Jung compared certain representations to the " . . . pattern of ideas, of a numinous or fascinating character, which . . . compels the moth to carry out its fertilizing activity on the yucca plant. . . ." (C.W. 10, par. 547).

Jung thus considered the image much more for its activity than for the representative elements that comprise it. The archetypal idea, then, approaches that of instinct.

> In any situation of panic, whether external or internal, the archetypes intervene and allow a man to react in an instinctively adapted way, just as if he had always known the situation: he reacts in the way mankind has always reacted. (C.W. 18, par. 368)

From Representations to Potentials

Another factor contributed to the evolution of Jung's thought. Very early on, Jung came across the question of the transmission of original images. If these fundamental representational schemes are at work everywhere and at all times, and if it seems unthinkable that they are invented anew in every situation, how then are they transmitted?

Jung believed that the theory of cultural and educational transmission inadequately explains his observations:

> But, in point of fact, typical mythologems were observed among individuals to whom all knowledge of this kind was absolutely out of the question, and where indirect derivation from religious ideas that might have been known to them, or from popular figures of speech, was impossible. Such conclusions forced us to assume that we must be dealing with "autochthonous" revivals independent of all tradition, and, consequently, that

"myth-forming" structural elements must be present in the unconscious psyche. (C.W. 9/1, par. 259)

He dismissed the "innate" hypothesis. His knowledge of anthropology forbade him, in fact, from supposing that representations can be transmitted genetically. Yet somehow, his reflections led him to affirm the following in 1921:

Contents of the collective unconscious [are] . . . residues, or "engrams". . . . (C.W. 7, par. 158)

The archetypes are as it were the hidden foundations of the conscious mind. . . . They are inherited with the brain structure—indeed, they are its psychic aspect. (C.W. 10, par. 53)

How can one simultaneously hold two apparently incompatible views: that representations are not innate and that original images are biologically inscribed? Jung hesitated to commit himself until he was helped along by an analogy taken from the development of animal behavior.

No biologist would ever dream of assuming that each individual acquires his general mode of behavior afresh each time. It is much more probable that the young weaver-bird builds his characteristic nest because he is a weaver bird and not a rabbit. Similarly, it is more probable that man is born with a specifically human mode of behavior and not with that of a hippopotamus or with none at all. (C.W. 8, par. 435)

Psychology can therefore find inspiration in the way biology frames the problem concerning the innateness or the transmission of certain ideas. It is not representations that are transmitted but the structures from which representations arise. This view allowed Jung to define the archetypes as "congenital structures."

Pattern of Behavior

Even if this idea of congenital structure is more satisfactory to Jung, the question of its nature still needs to be asked. However, around 1938 Jung came across an idea that seemed useful to him in defining congenital structures—the idea of *pattern of behavior*. He borrowed this concept from biology and continued to use it well into his later works, even though by then his thought had evolved beyond that idea. In his 1946 version of *Analytical Psychology and Education* (found in C.W. 18), Jung once again took up and explicated an earlier 1910 assertion relating to the topic of inherited systems, using the concept of *pattern of behavior*.

These inherited systems correspond to the human situations that have existed since primeval times. . . . I have called this congenital and preexistent instinctual model, or pattern of behavior, the archetype. (C.W. Vol. 4, par. 728)

Furthermore, in a text found in the 1952 version of *Symbols of Transformation*, he wrote:

> This observation was not an isolated case: it was manifestly not a question of inherited ideas, but of an inborn disposition to produce parallel thought-formations, or rather of identical psychic structures common to all men, which I later called the archetypes of the collective unconscious. (C.W. 5, par. 224)

Archetypal Images and Archetypes

By following the logic of the idea of the archetype, Jung was led to distinguish the archetypal image from the archetype *per se*. The pattern of the archetype is genetically transmitted, while the circumstances surrounding the archetype flesh it out into a particular image. It is at this latter level that culture plays a determining role.

In 1946 in his article "On the Nature of the Psyche" (C.W. VIII), Jung arrived at a decisive formulation of the archetype:

> The archetypal representations (images and ideas) mediated to us by the unconscious should not be confused with the archetype as such. They are very varied structures which all point back to one essentially "irrepresentable" basic form. . . . it seems to me probable that the real nature of the archetype is not capable of being made conscious. . . . (C.W. 8, par. 417)

> Whatever we say about the archetypes, they remain visualisations or concretizations which pertain to the field of consciousness. But—we cannot speak about archetypes in any other way. We must, however, constantly bear in mind that what we mean by "archetype" is in itself irrepresentable, but has effects which make visualizations of it possible, namely, the archetypal images and ideas (C.W. 8, par. 417)

From the above quotations, there follows this key idea:

> [The archetype] cannot be explained in just any way, but only in the one that is indicated by that particular individual. (C.W. 18, par. 589)

Organs of Information

Even while he resorted to using, successively, the notions of form, structure, living form, and finally pattern, Jung indicated from time to time another possible line of thought:

> [The archetypes are] a living system of reactions and aptitudes. . . . (C.W. 8, par. 339)

> Archetypes . . . are living entities. . . . (C.W. 18, par. 1272)

If the idea of pattern of behavior interested Jung, it was because this concept allowed him to make a link between unconscious psychological organizations, which he sought to understand, and what can be known of animal behavior. But the concept of pattern still bore too close a resemblance to the idea of model. Jung sensed that the "pattern" concept does not correspond exactly to that of "archetype."

He made several attempts to sketch out other ways of seeing the archetype:

> The archetypes are, so to speak, organs of the prerational psyche. (C.W. 11, par. 845)

> For the archetype is an element of our psychic structure and thus a vital and necessary component in our psychic economy. (C.W. 9/1, par. 271)

> [The archetype] is a self-activating organism, endowed with generative power. (C.W. 6, par. 754)

Jung's characterization of the archetype as organ is excellent because it reflects the archetype's constant activity and the role the archetype plays in the psychic apparatus. In addition, he compared the archetype to the eye, a comparison that precludes description of the archetype as model. Rather, archetypal images are as different from the archetype as optical images are different from the eye. Archetypal and optical images are formed by the relation that their respective organs have to the external object. At least twice in 1946, Jung resorted to another comparison that likens the archetype to the axial system which, while having no existence of its own, somehow directs ions and molecules as they form crystals.

In fact, Jung's thought began to hint at a concept that was not yet available in Jung's time: the concept of information. The role Jung attributed to archetypes is perfectly intelligible if one uses the concepts of information theory: (1) archetypes condition, orient, and support the formation of the individual psyche according to a plan that is inherent to them; (2) whenever the psyche is disturbed, archetypes intervene by considering information received either from the psyche itself or from the environment; (3) archetypes ensure an exchange of information between the psyche and its surroundings.

Let me add that for Jung—and he was not hesitant on this point—the archetypes are inscribed in the body in the same way that all organs of information are inscribed in living matter. This implies, among other things, that archetypes are genetically transmitted.

Retrospectively, it is interesting to note that the idea about the genetic transmission of archetypes is already expressed in a text dating back to 1921.

We are forced to assume that the given structure of the brain does not owe its peculiar nature merely to the influence of surrounding conditions, but also and just as much to the peculiar and autonomous quality of living matter, i.e., to a law inherent in life itself. The given constitution of the organism, therefore, is on the one hand a product of external conditions, while on the other it is determined by the intrinsic nature of living matter. (C.W. 6, par. 748)

There is nothing to prevent us from assuming that certain archetypes exist even in animals, that they are grounded in the peculiarities of the living organism itself and are therefore direct expressions of life whose nature cannot be further explained. (C.W. 7, par. 109)

Archetypes, Complexes, and Symbols

Having elaborated his theory this far, Jung asked two questions which we will take up one at a time: (1) What do the unconscious organizers do? (2) How are the unconscious organizers related to genetic factors?

The distinction Jung made between the archetypal image and archetype (illustrated by the comparison of the archetype to the eye) suggests that representations come about when unconscious patterns select data and put it into form. The same hypothesis holds for the formation of imagos, complexes, and the psychic apparatus, the latter being structured around the ego complex. Archetypal images, however, differ from these other psychic entities in one major way: when the individual psyche is constituted, it begets the unconscious. The agencies that make up the individual psyche remain, in fact, partially unconscious. Their coming into existence entails deficiencies, the consequences of which are equally unconscious; and the activity of these agencies can bring to consciousness only part of the information received. Thus an unconscious dynamic different from the archetypal one is developed and structured.

There are therefore two composite entities whose reasons for being unconscious are quite different. One belongs to the species, the other is the counterpart to individual consciousness. The constitution, functioning, and history of these entities are governed by laws proper to each.

The theoretical effort of psychoanalysis has focused principally upon those unconscious dynamics that result from the individual's personal life, most probably because analysands have usually been of the neurotic sort until fairly recently. Jung found himself in a very different situation. For many years, he head to treat psychotic patients in psychiatric wards. He had to deal not with dysfunctions, but with the suffering of psyches that had failed to achieve adequate organization. This experience led Jung to pay particular attention to the biological factors that might underly psychosis and to inquire into those archaic dynamics that are incomparably stronger than the conscious personality. Following a critical period in his own life, which we have already mentioned, Jung discovered within himself the same kind of dynamics he had observed in psychotics. He noticed, however, that these dynamics need not cause destruction, but that they could, on the contrary, exercise a positive influence. By confronting these dynamics, Jung observed that psychological growth comes from the unconscious. Jung's twofold experience of psychotic patients and of psychic maturation led him to surmise, in what he wrote between the years 1919 and 1923, that unconscious factors are at the source of both psychic illness and psychic healing.

How can archetypal factors be considered psychic organizers if they are responsible for psychic disturbances? Jung observed, first of all, that a representation, an affect, or an impulse is more powerful the less individualized it is and the more it resembles the reactions typical of many people. He concluded that these representations, or more elementary impulses, express more directly general situations and, therefore, psychic organizations that are valid for everyone. He called these organizations "collective" to indicate that the energy they have at their disposal and the forms to which they give life are what make us human. To the extent that life circumstances and especially heredity, the desire of one's parents, as well as social, cultural, and economic conditions do not allow a sufficiently strong conscious psyche to take up these collective dynamics, the personality risks being flooded or insiduously possessed by unconscious factors.

One can also observe in analytic therapy that consciousness can become caught in an ambivalence particularly evident in the bipolarity of images and of complexes. It can also be seen that consciousness evolves by differentiating the archetypes—for example, by differentiating the animus and the anima from their respective parental imagos. The inherent ambivalence of archetypes and their mutual contamination of each other contribute to the individual psyche's unfinished and disordered state.

The archetypes can therefore function as organizers only by virtue of the activity of conscious factors. They are, however, always present, as constant sources of information for consciousness. Through compensation, archetypes correct individual psychic disturbances and propose symbols that can give direction to the psyche.

The presence of archetypes justifies the therapeutic question as to whether it is possible to relate to unconscious organizing schemas such that they can have a positive influence on life. The search for an answer to that question is at the foundation of Jungian analysis. To become conscious not only consists in discovering and experiencing the mechanisms that simultaneously fashion and ensnare us, but also involves allowing that which can repair the psyche to do so. This is what is meant by the idea of "relation to the unconscious," an idea first brought to psychoanalysis by Jung.

Psychoid, Synchronicity, Unity of the World

> The direct perception of the archetypal world inside us is just as doubtfully correct as that of the physical world outside us. (C.W. 14, par. 787)

The archetypes are no more capable of being made conscious than the reality-in-itself of the universe. Archetypes and the universe are unknowable except through their activities. Everything goes on as if the psyche were not entirely able to assimilate the archetypes. They seem to be somehow "beyond" or "beneath" whatever is psychic in nature. This was what Jung meant by the term "psychoid."

> I have never been inclined to think that our senses were capable of perceiving all forms of being. I have, therefore, even hazarded the postulate that the phenomenon of archetypal configurations—which are psychic events par excellence—may be founded upon a psychoid base, that is, upon an only partially psychic and possibly altogether different form of being. (M.D.R., p. 351)

Jung asked himself, then, if an encounter with the psychoid nature of the archetypes might not occur in those surprising moments when external events coincide with corresponding psychic states.

The coincidences he noted, which he called "synchronistic phenomena," are not merely a sort of analogical play of dates, names, and places. Rather, the experience of synchronicity is an experience of time. Events correspond to subjective states in such a way that whoever is involved in the event is touched at the level of reality. The perception of the passage of time seems to be suspended in order to allow for the perception of another organization where as-yet-unknown dynamics are articulated according to a different set of laws. The significance of synchronistic pheonomena comes from the impression that not all of life can be explained merely in the framework of past-present-future, but that life also—one could say, rather—belongs to altogether another register. Concrete circumstances and psychic phenomena appear to be coordinated by a center that is outside the individual psyche.

To account for these synchronistic events, Jung proposed the hypothesis of a psycho-physical continuum. He introduced this continuum by comparing it to the light spectrum (C.W. 8, par. 367).

The psyche, which we tend to see as a subjective fact, extends outside of us, beyond time, beyond space. (E., pp. 540-1, tr. RGJ)

The deeper and more obscure these layers are, the more they lose their individual originality. The deeper they are, that is, the more they approach the functional autonomous systems, the more they become collective and universal and are extinguished in the materiality of the body, that is, in the chemical body. The carbon of the human body is simply carbon; at its deepest level, the psyche is but the universe. (I.E.M., p. 454, tr. RGJ)

Chapter 3

Consciousness and the Unconscious

Consciousness

To understand the lives of his patients, Jung arrived at the hypothesis of archetypes. He then applied this theoretical point of view to the study of human nature.

> Natural history tells us of a haphazard and casual transformation of species over hundreds of millions of years of devouring and being devoured. The biological and political history of man is an elaborate repetition of the same thing. But the history of the mind offers a different picture. Here the miracle of reflecting consciousness intervenes—the second cosmogony. (M.D.R., p. 339)

The world exists only by means of consciousness: "Human consciousness created objective existence and meaning, and man found his indispensable place in the great process of being" (M.D.R., p. 256).

It is through consciousness that meaning can be discerned. "In the final analysis, the decisive factor is always consciousness, which can understand the manifestations of the unconscious and take up a position toward them" (M.D.R., p. 187).

This is why ". . . therapy aims at strengthening the conscious mind . . ." (C.W. 16, par. 479).

However important it may be, consciousness is nonetheless fragile and limited.

> For indeed our consciousness does not create itself—it wells up from unknown depths. In childhood it awakens gradually, and all through life it wakes each morning out of the depths of sleep out of an unconscious con-

dition. It is like a child that is born daily out of primordial womb of the unconscious. (C.W. 11, par. 935)

The real and authentic psyche is the unconscious, whereas the ego-consciousness can be regarded only as a temporary epiphenomenon. (C.W. 16, par. 205)

Causes and ends thus transcend consciousness to a degree that ought not to be underestimated, and this implies that their nature and action are unalterable and irreversable so long as they have not become objects of consciousness. They can only be corrected through conscious insight and moral determination, which is why self-knowledge, being so necessary, is feared so much. (C.W. 9/2, par. 253)

The task of becoming conscious is universal in scope, yet it consists of self-knowledge. Jung always saw consciousness as a function of the subject.

No content can be conscious unless it is represented to a subject. (C.W. 9/2, par. 1)

Consciousness is therefore defined along two dimensions:

1) Relative to the whole psyche, ". . . consciousness is an inward perception of the objective life-process" (C.W. 8, par. 277). The German term that Jung used for intuition, *Anschauung*, highlights the fact that consciousness consists of the life-process reflecting upon itself.

2) Relative to the subject, "consciousness consists in the relation of a psychic content to the ego. Anything not associated with the ego remains unconscious" (C.W. 14, n. 400).

The existence of these two dimensions explains why the expansion of consciousness brings about a transformation of the subject. The withdrawal of projections and increasing consciousness of the shadow throw the ego into a state of conflict.

The progressive development and differentiation of consciousness . . . involves nothing less than a crucifixion of the ego. . . . (C.W. 9/2, par. 79)

Becoming Conscious

Because the conscious field is the function of a subject that hardly exists at the beginning of its history, and, secondly, because it is performed by the life-process reflecting upon itself—a process about which we know virtually nothing—this conscious field lacks clear boundaries. The conscious field is analogical, that is to say, psychic dynamics are "more or less" conscious, and thus conscious structures differ from one another in degrees of consciousness.

Between "I do this" and "I am conscious of doing this" there is a world of difference, amounting sometimes to outright contradiction. Consequently, there is a consciousness in which unconsciousness predominates, as well as a consciousness in which self-consciousness predominates. This paradox becomes immediately intelligible when we realize there is no conscious content which can with absolute certainty be said to be totally conscious, for that would necessitate an unimaginable totality of consciousness, and that in turn would presuppose an equally unimaginable wholeness and perfection of the human mind. So we come to the paradoxical conclusion that there is no conscious content which is not in some other respect unconscious. Maybe, too, there is no unconscious psychism which is not at the same time conscious. (C.W. 8, par. 385)

Consciousness is the process of becoming-conscious. It is striking that Jung consistently chose one word to designate this becoming-conscious (*Bewustwerden*), while he used various words to refer to being-conscious (*Bewusstein*).

Becoming-conscious crosses over many thresholds, which ". . . presupposes a mode of observation in terms of energy, according to which consciousness of psychic contents is essentially dependent upon their intensity" (C.W. 8, par. 363) and upon their value (C.W. 8, par. 17). Consciousness is a system of perception; and the access consciousness has to perceptions depends upon the amount of energy that these perceptions have.

Still, consciousness needs to have the means of dealing with information. Jung analyzed what he termed "phenomena of reception" and called attention to the role apperceptive concepts play. Apperceptive concepts are primarily the content matter of sciences and of traditions, which the experience of each person subsequently shapes in that person's own way.

This explains numerous neurotic disturbances which arise from the fact that certain contents are constellated in the unconscious but cannot be assimilated owing to the lack of apperceptive concepts that would "grasp" them. (C.W. 9/2, par. 259)

As he studied the psyche's efforts towards greater consciousness, Jung distinguished between assimilation, which is ". . . the approximation of already constellated subjective material . . ." (C.W. 6, par. 685), and integration, which puts the ego on the spot and forces it to change. When the process of becoming conscious is in an "assimilation" mode, it most often ends up reinforcing a dominant complex. Inversely, when it is in an integration mode, it inflicts a lesion upon the ego (C.W. 16, par. 472) and arrives at a differentiated relationship: ". . . integrated; it is withdrawn from projection and has become perceptible as a determining psychic factor" (C.W. 11, par. 394).

To become conscious means to confront the unconscious with the need for differentiation:

> Differentiation is the essence, the *sine qua non* of consciousness. (C.W. 7, par. 329)

This observation led Jung to conclude that the categories of space and time, which are responsible for differences in consciousness, are "postulated" by consciousness. It also brought him to define more completely what he understood by consciousness, which he had earlier defined with reference to its connection to the whole psyche and to the subject. He henceforth recognized a third dimension within it: "Where there is no 'other,' or it does not yet exist, all possibility of consciousness ceases." (C.W. 9/2, par. 301)

Typology and Conscious Orientation

How does consciousness take in what is foreign to it? Jung began to reflect on this matter by observing the contrast between those patients suffering from hysteria and those afflicted with dementia praecox. It seemed to him that the distinction that was then made between extraversion, characteristic of hysteria, and introversion, descriptive of the schizophrenic state, expressed quite well the difference between the two psychic disorders.

He was later struck by the fact that, even though Freud and Adler were theoretically opposed to each other, both of their theories seemed equally valid. He attributed the break-up of the relationship between these two men to their inability to admit that their theoretical divergences were due to differences in conscious structures: Freud, the extravert, in opposition to Adler, the introvert.

Jung was particularly sensitive to this example because it allowed him to touch upon the importance of understanding what such differences consist of, thereby avoiding being duped by the way consciousness perceives what is foreign to it. The differences between Freud and Adler likewise gave him a first clue: consciousness receives data according to its own orientation, which is either introverted or extraverted (to use terms that express quite well these different orientations.)

One cannot then imagine consciousness to be passive, as if it were a blank slate. Nor can it be seen as a neutral function that would be the same for everyone, because there are two radically different attitudes: the extraverted and the introverted. The first characterizes a consciousness directed toward the external object, the second a consciousness directed toward the subject.

Two points must be made here for the sake of precision. First, extraversion and introversion characterize the structure of consciousness. These attitudes are not meant to characterize behavior. One can meet contemplative monks who are extraverted and businessmen who are introverted. Jung was not always explicit about what he understood by object and subject, but his "object" seems to correspond to entities found in the exterior world, insofar as both the interior and the exterior worlds are objective realities.

Second, the introvert is not necessarily any more narcissistic than the extravert. They are simply not narcissistic in the same way, for the subjectivity of the first becomes intertwined with interior perceptions, while that of the second is projected out upon the concrete world.

Consciousness is then structured in accordance with either one of these two major systems of information, one external, the other internal. How is information subsequently sorted out? Jung went on to distinguish four aspects to this gathering of information: ". . . to establish that something exists . . . tell us what it means . . . what is its value . . . whence it comes and whither it goes . . . (C.W. 6, par. 983). Each aspect can be apprehended by a particular function, which he named in the following order: sensation (*Empfindung*), thought (*Verstand*), feeling (*Gefühl*), and intuition (*Intuition*).

Given that consciousness is focused, one of the psyche's four functions gains ascendancy over the others, either because the subject has an innate predisposition for that particular function or because that function above all others has proved most useful for the subject in early childhood. Consciousness is subsequently oriented consistently by this dominant function. That is to say, consciousness sorts out the information it receives from the world and does so according to the point of view that is congruent with its own dominant type.

There are, therefore, eight possible types of conscious orientations, if we combine introversion and extraversion with the four functions. The important point here, however, is not the classification of types. The value of Jung's typology lies in the dynamism it implies and in the tensions it brings to light.

In fact, if consciousness is oriented by a particular type, the type opposite the dominant one remains "floating," in that it is not bound to the ego. It is through the least dominant function that the most autonomous action of the unconscious will arise, true to the law of compensation. Psychological change and development will occur by means of this opposite function, which Jung called the inferior function. For example, the inferior function of the introverted thinker is in the area of extraverted feeling.

I cannot, within the scope of this analysis hope to do justice to the dynamics that pertain to Jung's typology, in the same way that I was unable to present the clinical aspects of the shadow, the animus and the anima, and of the Self. I only want to call attention to the tremendous practical usefulness of Jung's typology. In clinical consultation, the diagnosis of the primary and of the secondary functions not only allows for an understanding of how patients perceive the world and orient themselves in it, but also clarifies the conditions under which patients can mature.

In the course of an analysis, transference takes place and is transformed within a framework that is determined by the similarity, the complementarity, or the opposition of the analyst's conscious structure to that of the analysand. It has been observed that the source of differences and instability in the analytic relationship lies in a typological opposition between the analyst and the analysand, or that a collusion that is difficult to overcome can be attributed to a typological similarity between them.

The Unconscious

> Because the unconscious, in fact and by definition, cannot be discriminated as such, the most we can hope to do is to infer its nature from the empirical material. (C.W. 11, par. 419)

After he had approached consciousness from the perspective of the archetypes, in a very characteristic move Jung inverted the meaning of the subject-object relationship and examined the unconscious from the vantage point of consciousness.

> Theoretically, no limits can be set to the field of consciousness, since it is capable of indefinite extension. Empirically, however, it always finds its limit when it comes up against the unknown. This consists of everything we do not know, which, therefore, is not related to the ego as the center of the field of consciousness. The unknown falls into two groups of objects: those which are outside and can be experienced by the senses and those which are inside and are experienced immediately. The first group comprises the unknown in the outer world; the second the unknown in the inner world. We call this latter territory the unconscious. (C.W. 9/2, par. 2)

Jung defined the unconscious by its contents, whereas he had earlier defined consciousness by its role. We will next see how he viewed the role of the unconscious.

> The unconscious has still another side to it: it includes not only repressed contents, but all psychic material that lies below the threshold of consciousness. (C.W. 7, par. 203)

From the point of view of the psychology of consciousness, one can distinguish three types of unconscious contents, according to whether they: 1. are temporarily subliminal, but can be made conscious through an act of will; 2. cannot be made conscious through an act of will; or 3. cannot be made conscious at all.

Personal Unconscious — Collective Unconscious

Whatever interest he might have in studying all three types of unconscious contents and the problems that each raises, Jung set out, in particular, to analyze the manifestations of the unconscious in terms of a psychology of personality. This undertaking led him to distinguish between the personal and the collective unconscious.

> Whereas the contents of the personal unconscious are acquired during the individual's lifetime, the contents of the collective unconscious are invariably archetypes that were present from the beginning. (C.W. 9/2, par. 13)

From the clinical standpoint, Jung is more precise:

> We distinguish between a personal unconscious which enables us to recognize the shadow and an impersonal unconscious which enables us to recognize the archetypal symbol of the self. (C.W. 9/2, par. 261)

What we have already said of archetypes brings us to the discussion of the spatial metaphor that has been used to represent the personal and the collective unconscious as two superimposed strata. The personal unconscious is made from the collective unconscious. In fact, it results from the convergence of the sources of information that govern human development and takes into consideration the circumstances, particularities, choices, heredity, and traditions — in the final analysis, all of the physical and psychical contexts of existence, social as well as individual. It is this phenomenon that psychoanalysis initially grasped and that Freud elaborated. Jung went further than Freud, explicating the manifestations of the unconscious and concluding with his hypothesis of the existence of the archetype. That Jung, a pioneer, was engulfed by the theory of the archetype does not diminish in the slightest the reality and the importance of personal unconscious formations. Any analyst who bypasses the personal unconscious in order to reach the collective unconscious more quickly will provoke an inflation in the analysand. In fact, under such circumstances the analysand will not be able to confront the collective unconscious through a profound, personal experience — the kind of experience about which Jung spoke. Instead, the analysand will be left only with a reflection of the collective unconscious within his or her own imagination.

Any analysis that neglects the experience of the collective dimensions of the unconscious appears an absurd mutilation of the psyche. But this experience of the collective unconscious nonetheless attests to the value of a statement Jung repeated often: there is no other way than that of self-knowledge.

The Collective Unconscious

Whereas the principal formations of the personal unconscious are imagos and complexes, the collective unconscious consists "of the sum of the instincts and their correlates, the archetypes" (C.W. 8, par. 281).

Jung's work is rooted within the reflection that brought him to the idea of the archetype. For that reason, we presented the chapter on the archetypes separately. If we take a global perspective of the collective unconscious, we have to speak of a factor to which Jung frequently referred, but which he never clearly defined: instinct, or the instincts. Is the reality of the instincts analogous to that of the Id? Are instincts a cluster of drives that constitute the dynamic substructure of the psyche? Jung did not say. When he spoke about instincts, he referred to a mode of behavior whose ability to adapt is governed by an internal unconscious goal-directedness. This goal-directedness is established either by happenstance or by selection. The notion of instinct connoted, for Jung, both a continuity between psychic and biological realms, as well as an automatism and a subjectivity. He wrote for example:

> . . . the qualities which are the hallmarks of instinct: automatism, non-susceptibility to influence, all-or-none reaction, and so forth. (C.W. 8, par. 384)

The rigidity of the instincts is at the origin of the repetitive and compulsive nature of the complexes' effects upon consciousness.

In a general way the idea of collective unconscious harkens back to that of the unconscious psyche: ". . . through our unconscious, we have a share in the historical collective psyche . . ." (C.W. 7, par. 150).

Jung observed that certain unconscious dynamics do not arise from subjectivity and follow a law that is all their own.

> This idea of the independence of the unconscious, which distinguishes my views so radically from those of Freud, came to me as far back as 1902, when I was engaged in studying the psychic history of a young girl somnambulist. (C.W. 7, preface)

The unconscious is an objective reality, that is, it is just as independent of individual subjectivity as the outer world; and this is how Jung first characterized objective reality in his theory. The collective unconscious is ". . . identical in all men and thus constitutes a common psychic substrate of a suprapersonal nature which is present in every one of us" (C.W. 9/1, par. 3).

The unconscious is also characterized by its creative activity, in the sense that the dynamics that make us human are not conscious.

> For me the unconscious is a collective psychic disposition, creative in character. (C.W. 11, par. 875)

> The unconscious is the matrix of all metaphysical statements, of all mythology, of all philosophy (so far as this is not merely critical), and of all expressions of life that are based on psychological premises. (C.W. 11, par. 899)

To the extent that the unconscious dynamics are not chaotic but are, on the contrary, responsible for the world of forms and relatively ordered associations, one is led to believe there is an unconscious form of knowing. This conjecture is confirmed in particular by the way in which dreams bring to the fabric of life information that is often more appropriate and penetrating than information given by consciousness. Furthermore, based on synchronistic phenomena, Jung stated that unconscious knowledge has an "absolute" character insofar as it is relatively independent of space and time.

> However incomprehensible it may appear, we are finally compelled to assume that there is in the unconscious something like an a priori knowledge or an "immediacy" of events which lacks any causal basis. (C.W. 8, par. 856)

In summary, Jung defined the unconscious as an objective reality that is the seat of creativity and of the processes that could be called, using the language of consciousness, knowledge. He observed that the unconscious dynamics remain structurely ambivalent and contaminated, that is, they can easily be reversed, one extreme turning into its opposite. It is in response to this proclivity to reversal and confusion that consciousness insists upon the task of differentiation.

The Conscious-Unconscious Structure

Jung saw the relationship between consciousness and the unconscious as a structure.

> But all effects are mutual, and nothing changes anything else without itself being changed. (C.W. 14, par. 764)

It is this structure that he called *psyche* (C.W. 8, par. 397). He defined psyche as "wholeness" in order to emphasize—by referring to both meanings of the word *Ganzheit*—that each person's possibility for becoming himself or herself depends upon the functioning of this psychic structure.

If consciousness develops by cutting itself off from the unconscious, the personal unconscious formations regress and lose their adaptability to the conscious world. They thus become more and more rigid and negative. Moreover, the compensation that emanates from the collective unconscious becomes that much more discordant with, and unacceptable to, consciousness.

If the process of becoming conscious occurs in harmony with unconscious dynamics, unconscious development then becomes more precise and better adapted to life.

> The unconscious functions satisfactorily only when the conscious mind fulfils its tasks to the very limit. (C.W. 8, par. 568)

For Jung, the aim of becoming conscious, therefore, is not to absorb the unconscious but to allow psychic structures to function satisfactorily. A satisfactorily functioning psyche implies an exchange between consciousness and the unconscious, the optimal level of which will vary greatly from one individual to another, but which is, in any case, at the basis of each person's psychic health.

Chapter 4

The Individuation Process

[The] growth of personality comes out of the unconscious. . . . (C.W. 11, par. 390)

This statement has many implications. It suggests a certain attitude toward life, and it affects one's concept of therapy. It is the logical outgrowth of a Jungian approach to the psyche which leads one to confront oneself and, ultimately, to encounter collective unconscious dynamism.

Given that they are an ever-present source of information, archetypes act in a constant fashion. Everyone is affected by their influence and can be changed by them. But in what way do the archetypes exercise their influence? How can the subject be receptive to and integrate an archetype, given that he or she is limited by circumstances, natural abilities, and the conditions resulting from childhood and adolescence?

It was between the years 1912 and 1918 that Jung first observed archetypes at work within himself. He gradually conceived of archetypes as growth processes, which one could characterize as processes of humanization. Jung called this process "individuation," not because the individual is, properly speaking, at the center of the process, but because the relationship of the individual to the collective (in the sense already defined) assumes and transcends the subject-object dichotomy.

Through the study of these collective transformation processees and through understanding of alchemical symbolism, I arrived at the central concept of my psychology: the process of individuation. (M.D.R., p. 209)

In "The Relations Between the Ego and the Unconscious" I had discussed only my preoccupation with the unconscious, and something of the nature of that preoccupation, but had not yet said anything much about the unconscious itself. As I worked with my fantasies, I became aware that the unconscious undergoes or produces change. Only after I had familiarized myself with alchemy did I realize that the unconscious is a process, and

115

that the psyche is transformed or developed by the relationship of the ego to the contents of the unconscious. In individual cases that transformation can be read from dreams and fantasies. In collective life it has left its deposit principally in the various religious systems and their changing symbols. (M.D.R., p. 209)

The Idea of Individuation

The idea of a principle of individuation appears, probably for the first time in Jung's work, in 1916 in the *Seven Sermons to the Dead* and in an essay, "Adaptation, Individuation, and Collectivity" (C.W. 18). The idea of individuation finds its sources in Schopenhauer as well as in the Goethian *Bildungsroman*. Jung, however, radically transformed the idea of individuation by basing it on the long adventure of the ego's relations to the Self and upon his own experience of mandala imagery.

> I use the term "individuation" to denote the process by which a person becomes a psychological "in-dividual," that is, a separate indivisible unity or "whole". (C.W. 11, par. 490)

This is the implicit goal of the unconscious dynamics.

> We know that the unconscious goes straight for its goal and that this does not consist solely in pairing two animals but in allowing an individual to become whole (*ganz werden*). (C.W. 9/1, par. 540)

The dynamic upon which this aim is based presents itself to consciousness in various images of the Self. Jung at times called this dynamic "instinct" in order to emphasize that it consists of a "natural and impersonal process"; at other times, he called it "Logos," in order to indicate that this process adheres to and creates an intelligible order.

> It is the ascendency of the "complete" . . . or total human being, consisting of the totality of the psyche, of conscious and unconscious, over the ego, which represents only consciousness and its contents and knows nothing of the unconscious, although in many respects it is dependent on the unconscious and is often decisively influenced by it. (C.W. 12, par. 713)

> Insofar as this process, as a rule, runs its course unconsciously as it has from time immemorial, it means no more than that the acorn becomes an oak, the calf a cow, and the child an adult. But if the individuation process is made conscious, consciousness must confront the unconscious and the balance between the opposites must be found. As this is not possible through logic, one is dependent upon symbols which make the irrational union of opposites possible. They are produced spontaneously by the unconscious and are amplified by the conscious mind. (C.W. 11, par. 755)

When it takes place unconsciously, the individuation process is projected upon collective symbols, myths, religions, and philosophies, which inspire those who believe in them. But then ". . . the end remains as dark as the beginning" (C.W. 11, par. 756). On the other hand, when the process becomes conscious ". . . so much darkness comes to light, and consciousness necessarily gains in scope and insight" (C.W. 11, par. 756).

Individuation can then be seen as an unconscious process that underlies the flow of life and is transformed when it becomes conscious, that is, in Jung's view, when the ego experiences the collective unconscious. A distinction should be made between an unconscious individuation, which results from a natural symbolic process, and a personal individuation, which takes place as a consequence of an individual confrontation with that symbolic process. The ego experiences the collective unconscious when it encounters the shadow or when the animus and the anima are differentiated from the external images upon which they were originally projected. Individuation always takes the form of a conflict by which the subject is transformed.

> To one familiar with our psychology, it may seem a waste of time to keep harping on the long-established difference between becoming conscious and the coming-to-be of the self (individuation). But again and again I note that the individuation process is confused with the coming of the ego into consciousness and that the ego is in consequence identified with the self, which naturally produces a hopeless conceptual muddle. Individuation is then nothing but ego-centeredness and autoeroticism. (C.W. 7, par. 432)

Individuation presupposes that the ego has recognized and come to terms with the unconscious center of the personality. Jung was referring to that center when he used the phrase "being whole." Wholeness results from the coordination of the ego with the Self, whatever may be the subject's wounds and lacks. This is so because wholeness does not mean having or being everything; it means, rather, living in a structure within which opposites are at play.

Jung observed that the archetypal image of the quaternity best expresses this structure. He studied this archetype as he came across it in numerous historical and clinical documents and was led to conclude that it had two principal forms. The first, the "dual couple" (as, for example, in the transference which involves the analyst-analysand and the animus-anima), explicates and coordinates related factors present within a given situation. The second form is the image of the "three plus one" (as, for example, in typology, where three functions are attached to the ego and one remains unconscious), which expresses far better than the image of the "dual couple" those situations within which there is psychological movement. When they are well utilized, these formulae can generate hypotheses. They draw attention to the probable evolution of the structures that underlie apparently unrelated psychic phenomena.

A quaternity image of individuation on which Jung particularly focused is the image of the cross. It expresses psychological development as well as psychological conflict and integration. The individuating psyche is indivisible—that is, integrated—because it holds opposites together. The psyche becomes more itself by becoming more centered, but it does so without isolating itself from others.

The differentiation of the individual from the collective, in the sense that this differentiation was defined by Jung, connects human beings to their environment rather than severing them from it. Individuation is the opposite of individualism.

> Individuation does not shut one out from the world, but gathers the world to oneself. (C.W. 8, par. 432)

> Individuation has two principal aspects: in the first place it is an internal and subjective process of integration, and in the second it is an equally indispensible process of objective relationship. Neither can exist without the other, although sometimes the one and sometimes the other predominates. (C.W. 16, par. 448)

Projections and Possessions

The word individuation suggests an ongoing process. It may well be that this process is a never-ending one.

It refers, in fact, to an original state that is not to be confused with beginnings. Jung called this state "archaic identity" or "participation mystique," a term that he borrowed from Levy-Bruhl. Jung defined this as the non-differentiation of the subject and the object: "The psyche is initially the world." While this state corresponds to the initial stages of psychic life, it is nonetheless true that sectors of this kind persist in the adult psyche. To that extent, origins are always present.

Consciousness generally lives a life based on evidence, that is, it identifies what it experiences, or what it thinks, with what it takes to be real. It is thus "possessed" by the unconscious forces that individual circumstances bring into play. Consciousness however also benefits from an energy that is not its own. This energy comes in part from the archetypes and in part from social interactions. The personality is doubly bound in by the external and the internal worlds, and it unconsciously perceives that it owes its life energy to its own lack of differentiation.

Failure or pathology forces one to ask questions. Because there is suffering, archaic identity has a chance of being dismantled. The individual, who is then on the spot, might be able to get unstuck from what he or she has taken for granted. While a subject-object field is being constituted, consciousness discovers that what it took to be real was "a part of the subject transferred upon an object," a projection.

Recognizing and withdrawing projections first of all leads the individual to experience a feeling of emptiness, a disenchantment, or a loss of the wonderful. On the other hand, it also returns energy to consciousness and, more precisely, to the ego. This produces an "extension of the personality," which Jung called inflation.

> The man who recognizes his shadow knows very well that he is not harmless, for it brings the archaic psyche, the whole world of the archetypes, into direct contact with the conscious mind and saturates it with archaic influences. (C.W. 16, par. 452)

Becoming conscious of projections thus brings about inflation. Throughout his writings, Jung called attention to the dissolution of consciousness brought about by inflation. An inflation is all the more inevitable as psychic phenomena appear to consciousness in the best possible light. A feeling of freedom and renewed energy replace the unpleasant feelings that had been part of analysis up until that time. Analysands feel a willingness and a capacity to face up to life, and they are then tempted to leave analysis altogether. In fact, it is well known that, under such circumstances, this upsurge of energy is hardly integrated; it is actually dependent upon the dynamics with which the ego remains identified. Indications that the ego has identified with projections are evident in the subject's uncertainty about limits, quick reversals of opinions and behavior, and in states where elation alternates with depression, all of which characterize the unconscious. These states summarize what Jung called positive and negative inflations.

It may then happen that analysands discontinue analysis because of the benefit they derive from the energy that inflation imparts. Nonetheless, the activity of the anima or the animus then becomes unbearable, and once again the subject is thrust into questioning. This questioning bears upon the nature of the forces with which the ego has identified, and it leads the ego to recognize the collective characteristics of these forces.

For Jung, the process that finds its beginnings in archaic identity and in a state of possession, therefore, goes through two phases. First, the ego separates from the outer world by withdrawing projections. Second, the ego separates from the inner world by making ego inflation conscious and by objectifying the archetypal nature of the collective unconscious forces.

Incest and Sacrifice

The detachment of projections and the decrease of inflation take place by means of painful ruptures, which entail gradual and clearer recognition of the limits of the personality. Jung analyzed this process at length in his *Symbols of Transformation* (1911-1912). He later referred to this process frequently, in particular in *Psychology and Alchemy* and in his essay "Transformation Symbolism in the Mass."

To speak of these necessary ruptures, Jung used the term "sacrifice," a term that has referred to such psychological ruptures for millenia. "Sacrifice" clearly underscores the fact that separation, mourning, and castration are not merely severances and losses, but, provided they are fully lived out, belong to the process of transformation. The Miss Miller case, which Jung studied in *Symbols of Transformation*, induced him to emphasize the necessity of separating oneself from first attachments if one is to adapt to reality. "The natural course of life demands that the young person should sacrifice his childhood and his childish dependence on the physical parents . . ." (C.W. 5, par. 553). Detachment does not occur only at a set time nor relate only to first separations; it also has relevance for adults. It strikes against the ". . . bonds of unconscious incest. . . ," which are deleterious for "body and soul" (C.W. 5, par. 553) and which ". . . the unconscious will then re-create . . . all over again . . ." (C.W. 5, par. 644).

In order to liberate oneself from unconscious incest, one must sacrifice the infantile hero or the ideal ego within which "the conscious and unconscious fantasies" of the mother take form (C.W. 5, par. 461). One must also sacrifice ". . . the retrospective longing which only wants to resuscitate the torpid bliss and effortlessness of childhood . . ." (C.W. 5, par. 643). *

From the beginning, Jung analyzed sacrifice in relationship to the mother, whether this mother be the natural mother, the mother imago, or the Great Mother archetype. Putting to death the hero with whom Miss Miller felt identified ". . . means giving up the connection with the

---

*The ideal ego is clearly differentiated from the ego ideal. Both are narcissistic formations. The first, the ideal ego, corresponds to an identification of the ego with its own archaic representation. If either the ideal ego or the ego ideal persists into adulthood, the former becomes part of a borderline or psychotic structure, while the latter is associated with a neurotic structure.

mother, relinquishing all the ties and limitations which the psyche has taken over from childhood into adult life" (C.W. 5, par. 461). Emotional bonds and limitations enfold the individual in a non-differentiated state.

> For him who looks backwards the whole world, even the starry sky, becomes the mother who bends over him and enfolds him on all sides . . . as the all-encompassing world-soul Purusha has a maternal character, for he represents the original "dawn state" of the psyche: he is the encompassor and the encompassed, mother and unborn child, an undifferentiated, unconscious state of primal being. As such a condition must be terminated, and as it is at the same time an object of regressive longing, it must be sacrificed in order that discriminated entities—i.e., conscious contents—may come into being. (C.W. 5, par. 646).*

This is why sacrifice is not merely separation but also the prerequisite for the birth of the world.

> To the extent that the world and everything in it is a product of thought, the sacrifice of the libido that strives back to the past necessarily results in the creation of the world. (C.W. 5, par. 646)

> The world comes into being when man discovers it. But he only discovers it when he sacrifices his containment in the primal mother, the original state of unconsciousness. (C.W. 5, par. 652)

> From the renunciation of this image, and of the longing for it, arises the picture of the world as we know it today. (C.W. 5, par. 646)

Each time that a world, or an image of the world, is constituted, the individual tends to become enveloped in a dynamic of inclusion, that is, in the archetype of the Great Mother. This phenomenon can be found at different levels in the quest for the power of Desire, such as can be found in the cocoon of narcissism and in rationalism. It is in these areas that Jung saw the hold that the maternal imago can have over us.

The momentum of life can demand that these confinements be torn apart at one time or another. The history of myths illustrates the successive breaks from these states of psychological confinement.

> Comparison between the Mithraic and the Christian sacrifice should show just where the superiority of the Christian symbol lies: it lies in the frank admission that not only has man's animal instinctuality (symbolized by the bull) to be sacrificed, but the entire natural man, who is more than can be expressed by his theriomorphic symbol. (C.W. 5, par. 673)

---

*Purusha is, according to the *Rig-Veda*, the Primordial Being, the potentiality for everything that has been and will be.

The sacrifice of the "natural man," which the death of Christ symbolizes, signified for Jung the awareness at which the empirical investigations of analytical psychology are arriving today. This awareness is founded in the recognition that the ego must renounce all attempts to appropriate unconscious dynamics. The reason for this renunciation is that sacrifice brings about a change in the orientation of libido. It allows libido to regress into the unconscious and thereby makes it possible for new forms to emerge. Jung commented in the following manner upon the sacrifice of the cosmic horse found in the *Upanishads*:

> The horse-sacrifice signifies a renunciation of the world. . . . The sacrifice of the horse can only produce another phase of introversion similar to that which prevailed before the creation of the world. (C.W. 5, par. 658)

> We saw earlier on that the "mother-libido" must be sacrificed in order to create the world: here the world is destroyed by the renewed sacrifice of the same libido. . . . (C.W. 5, par. 658)

A comparison can be drawn between this conception of sacrifice and the idea of symbolic castration. A major difference between these two remains, however, because for Jung, the object-cathexis implied by both concepts does not have the final word, insofar as the idea of sacrifice further connotes access to the collective unconscious.

> In the act of sacrifice consciousness gives up its power and possessions in the interests of the unconscious. This makes possible a union of opposites resulting in a release of energy. (C.W. 5, par. 671)

What Jung called "union" is in fact a coming together of opposites, which excludes any idea that consciousness is isolated from its unconscious roots or that consciousness is possessed by the unconscious. Losses and separations liberate the conscious personality from identifications and predispose it to participate in whatever the unconscious proposes, without threat of its falling into alienation. In this sense, the return to the mother, to everlasting origins, must compensate for the sacrifice and the losses it demands.

> At this stage the mother-symbol no longer connects back to the beginnings, but points towards the unconscious as the creative matrix of the future. "Entry into the mother" then means establishing a relationship between the ego and the unconscious. (C.W. 5, par. 459)

With this view of the unconscious as a creative matrix, the question of incest must once again be taken up. Analysis discloses the incestuous wish and ascertains its strength in everyone; but once it has cleared the way for this repressed desire, it must not stop at having the wish for incest butt up against the incest prohibition or the practical impossibility of its being acted out. Jung categorically upheld the need for the incest prohibition (C.W. 5, par. 254), yet he observed that the problematic nature of incest was not yet overcome.

He wrote about this topic mainly in three works: *Symbols of Transformation* (1911 and 1952), the *Psychology of the Transference* (1946), and *Mysterium Coniunctionis* (1956). He investigated incest as a return to the mother in the first work, as an organizer of the transference in the second, and as the model of differentiation and conjunction in the third.

In contrast to the incest taboo prominent in almost all societies, there is a collection of myths, stories, and philosophical and theological themes in which incest plays a cosmogonic role. The situation extends further in some royal and priestly rituals during which incest was actually consummated. If one is to suppose (though it is far from being proven) that incestuous myths and rites are sublimations caused by the incest taboo, they nonetheless still present incest as having traits, context, development, and effects with very specific meaning. Might it not be that one can best learn the psychological meaning of the incestuous wish from these myths and rituals?

That the child is sexually attracted to the parent of the opposite sex would be a truism if something else were not also projected within that phenomenon of attraction. It is as if, in the more or less loosely gathered compilation of images, behaviors, surroundings, and times that comprise the incestuous drama, the psyche had found the framework within which incest could be realized. This realization could happen in such a way as to transcend the apparent goals of incest, thereby conferring on it a different meaning and consequently endowing it with a considerable surcharge of attraction. Every individual lusts not only for father, mother, brother, or sister, but also for what would happen if a union with them were possible. The conditions that give rise to incest cannot sufficiently account for its full meaning.

What then does incest aim for? It strives to find the Same, that is, the unconscious. Whether incest involves relations between brother and sister, daughter and father, son and mother, all seek the Mother in the intimacy that binds them together. The actual fullfilment of the incestuous wish would, however, be an "acting-out," aborting a desire that has a completely different intention. Symbolically, the desire for incest leads back to the unconscious in much the same way that one returns to the mother after having separated from her.

The living relationship to the unconscious, which borrows the emotional tone and image of a return to the Mother, goes hand-in-hand with the constitution of the subject. Conjunction does not negate, but it does presume separation. It is possible to recover the unconscious creative forces only if the subject is willing to sacrifice, in the sense discussed above. Without sacrifice, the personality would certainly be puffed up with inflation and would finally fall into a state of regression.

The society that has evolved under the influence of psychoanalysis fears a return to the unconscious. This society clings to the incest taboo as an ultimate rampart on the defense against nature and an undifferentiated psychological state. Jung shared these fears, but he coped with them differently. Because he dealt with illusion and mystification as part of the problematical nature of possession, he could acknowledge the positive dynamic that a state of possession can express. Convinced by his experience of the potentially positive side of possession, he refused to confine psychoanalysis to an art of frustration and criticism. He spoke frankly of the Mother and proposed to keep track of the living rhythm of separation from and reunion with her.

The Conjunction of Opposites

The conjunction of opposites is frequently misunderstood. For some people, conjunction means the juxtaposition of more or less contradictory attitudes; for others, it means the avoidance of conflict; and for others still, it suggests a play of conversion between the symmetrical versions of the Same. When one returns to Jung's original experience, it becomes apparent that conjunction involves something completely different from what any of these views suggest.

The fundamental paradox in the conjunction of opposites can be expressed in this way: vitality, a taste for living, the meaning of life— all flow from a participation with the unconscious, *provided* that the subject is differentiated and has broken off with precisely this same participation.

How can one resolve this paradox? The unconscious dynamics suggest a way out by opposing the impetus for growth, which demands sacrifice, to the desire for incest, which implies stagnation. Unconscious dynamics also oppose identification, which makes a symbol available to the subject, to compensation, which places this identification in question.

In the absence of a subject, these opposing dynamics remain chaotic and, once they reach a compromise with their opposites, are projected upon religions and ideologies. If one makes them conscious and understands them, on the other hand, they enter history. Whoever manages to hold opposing movements together is transformed by them. Jung was thus able to write: "[The] union of opposites . . . is the motivating force and the goal of the individuation process" (C.W. 13, par. 307).

By relating this text to those where Jung stated that the union of opposites is the unconscious state of origin, one can outline psychic evolution. The human being evolves from a conjunction-syzygy, whose opposing poles cannot exist without another, to a differentiated organization. The psyche is then simultaneously capable of relationships with persons of both the same and opposite sex, of introversion and extraversion, of faithfulness and betrayal—not by juxtaposing one state with another or by alternating from one state to the other, but by holding the opposites together within a unified subject.

In *Mysterium Coniunctionis*, Jung studied three successive conjunctions which he believed to be particularly significant: (1.) the conjunction of the soul with the spirit; (2.) the conjunction of the united soul and spirit with the body; (3.) the conjunction of the united psyche and body with the unity of the world.

Self-Regulation—Transcendent Function

> He can meet the demands of outer necessity in an ideal way only if he is also adapted to his own inner world, that is, if he is in harmony with himself. Conversely, he can only adapt to his inner world and achieve harmony with himself when he is adapted to the environmental conditions. (C.W. 8, par. 75)
>
> Individuation, becoming a self . . . is the problem of all life. (C.W. 12, par. 163)

In order to ensure life, our human nature has at its disposal an internal quasi-autonomous regulator, provided one manages to set it up. Education, psychotherapy, and maturity must allow for this possibility.

The self-regulation Jung spoke about does not pertain to homeostasis, whose net result would lead to stagnation. Self-regulation presupposes that multiple psychic factors are organized in such a way that a compensatory interplay can occur among them. The process by which the psyche finds equilibrium and orients itself occurs between the ego and the unconscious, at the level of drives as much as complexes. Self-regulation is each person's own. It varies from one moment to the next. It always remains problematic because it is achieved only gradually and only after many conflicts.

From 1916 on, Jung had the intuition that self-regulation was possible; and he began to explore this possibility in his essay "The Transcendent Function." The transcendence to which the title refers has nothing to do with metaphysics. Jung borrowed the term from mathematics and used it to designate an ability to shape psychic reality, made possible in a two-fold process: first, one makes unconscious factors speak, then one reacts to these unconscious factors by way of the ego's values and goals. An organization in tension, capable of proposing a new orientation to consciousness, is gradually substituted for resultant conflicts, particularly those that emerge between ego and shadow. This organization can appear as an inclination—a sort of inner voice, or as a symbol. Jung insisted much more upon this second, symbolic aspect; and it led him to say that there can be no individuation without symbols.

The transcendent function, which plays the role of an autonomous regulator, emerges and gradually begins to work as the process of individuation begins to unfold. For Jung, it is in the activation of the transcendent function that true maturity lies.

We have sometimes projected images of the hero upon this process. These images are childish. We have seen in fact how Jung denounced the hero's dependence upon the mother and affirmed the need to be freed from her. When he described the process of individuation, Jung intended to define an orientation and clarify that orientation's therapeutic and maturational possibilities, rather than to propose a model. To someone who had written to him inquiring about this topic, Jung replied:

> I must call your attention to the fact that I cannot possibly tell you what a man who has enjoyed complete self-realization looks like, and what becomes of him. I have never seen one. . . . Before we strive after perfection, we ought to be able to live the ordinary man without self-mutilation. (J. L. II, p. 474)

Chapter 5

Analysis

In order to become conscious of oneself, one needs another person. The individuation process does not evolve in solitude. Furthermore, the term "individual" does not mean "isolated"; it is rather derived from "undivided." Isolation is the consequence of an undifferentiated state, which is characterized by fusion with another and possession by the unconscious. Jung showed how the subject is constituted through a process of differentiation. The subject simultaneously separates from and forms bonds to others. Jung also showed that the relationship with another and the relationship with the unconscious are interrelated because both relationships are governed by the same function, the animus or the anima.

Even though Jung devoted the better part of his writings to the analysis of the subject's relation to the collective unconscious, he nonetheless regularly affirmed the concomitant importance of the relations to other human beings. Relationships with others was the object of one of his greatest books, *The Psychology of the Transference*. Furthermore, he described the mediators to the unconscious in sexual terms: the anima for the man and the animus for the woman. Contrary to what many advocate, the anima is not a model of the feminine, just as the animus is not a model of the masculine. Consequently, woman does not have an anima and man does not have an animus. Those who claim otherwise desexualize the mediating function and confuse man with the masculine and woman with the feminine.

Jung's conception of analysis is based upon the subject's relations to the inner and outer worlds. He does not separate the process of becoming conscious from the analytical relationship. It is by means of dialogue that one becomes conscious.

> The shadow can be realized only through a relation to a partner, and anima and animus only through a relation to a partner of the opposite sex,

because only in such a relation do their projections become operative. (C.W. 9/2, par. 42)

Psychotherapy is not the simple, straightforward method people at first believed it to be, but, as has generally become clear, a kind of dialectical process or discussion between two persons. Dialectic was originally the art of conversation among the ancient philosophers, but very early became the term for the process of creating new syntheses. (C.W. 16, par. 1)

Being an Analyst

Under such conditions, the personality of the analyst plays a deciding role. Jung once confided that he was aware that he conducted analysis by making use of who he himself was (see Percheron 1975). "The great healing factor in psychotherapy is the doctor's personality . . ." (C.W. 16, par. 198).

This observation suggests two others: (1) no one can help another person go further than one has gone oneself; (2) the personality of the person using the analytic method is more important that the method itself.

"If the wrong man uses the right means, the right means work in the wrong way." This Chinese saying, unfortunately only too true, stands in sharp contrast to our belief in the "right" method irrespective of the man who applies it. In reality, everything depends on the man and little or nothing on the method. (C.W. 13, par. 4)

It is from this perspective, when he was president of International Association of Psychoanalysts between 1910 and 1914, that Jung introduced the stipulation that all who wished to be analysts must first be analyzed themselves. Jung was thus the originator of the so-called didactic analysis. Aside from requiring in principle that future analysts undergo a didactic analysis, he emphasized the importance of knowledge and the role of the analyst's anima or animus. Knowledge and a relationship to the animus or anima are the two focal points of analytic training.

Knowledge prepares the analyst to discern signs. He or she must ally historical knowledge with clinical study:

Since . . . the symbols produced by the unconscious derive from archaic functioning, one must . . . have at one's command a vast amount of historical material; and, secondly, one must bring together and collate an equally large amount of empirical material based on direct observation. (C.W. 16, par. 253)

A mature animus or anima in the analyst's psyche ensures mediation of the unconscious by shielding the analyst from inflation. It ensures as well mediation for the patient in having the analyst respect the patient's own values (see Jung 1966 [H.D.A.], pp. 306-7).

The Sick Person

> The important thing is not the neurosis, but the man who has the neurosis. (C.W. 16, par. 190).

Jung clearly designates here the center of his therapeutic activity. From this perspective, the choice of which method to use in therapy is not determined by its intrinsic value but by its efficacy for a specific individual at a given moment. Of related interest is Jung's use of a vocabulary that does not distinguish between analysis and psychotherapy. He used the term *die Psychotherapie* to designate all kinds of psychotherapies, in contrast to physio- and chemotherapies. He distinguished the psychotherapies from each other according to whether or not they limited themselves to the healing of symptoms and whether or not they took the unconscious into consideration (refer, for example, to C.W. 16, par. 198).

Diagnosis is based on the subject's overall dynamics. Jung related the assessment of a psychic disturbance using the criteria of classical nosography to the role the disturbance plays in the subject's psychic economy and potential for integrating the disturbance. "[T]he medical picture of [the] disease is a provisional one. The real and important thing is the psychological picture, which can only be discovered in the course of treatment behind the veil of pathological symptoms" (C.W. 16, par. 210). Stated differently, what ultimately leads to a disgnostic decision is not merely the nature and severity of the symptoms but the state of the patient's complexes.

> In psychotherapy the recognition of the disease rests much less on the clinical picture than on the content of complexes. Psychological diagnosis aims at the diagnosis of complexes and hence at the formulation of facts which are far more likely to be concealed than revealed by the clinical picture. (C.W. 16, par. 196)

Jung took a comprehensive perspective to understand what makes people psychologically ill. "Insanity is possession by an unconscious content that, as such, is not assimilated to consciousness . . ." (C.W. 13, par. 53). In psychological illness, the relationship between consciousness and the unconscious is poor and archetypal information is unable to play its part correctly.

> When, therefore, the analysis penetrates the background of conscious phenomena, it discovers the same archetypal figures that activate the deleriums of psychotics. Finally, there is any amount of literary and historical evidence to prove that, in the case of these archetypes, we are dealing with normal types of fantasy that occur practically everywhere and not with the monstrous products of insanity. The pathological element does

not lie in the existence of ideas, but in the dissociation of consciousness
that can no longer control the unconscious. (C.W. 9/1, par. 83)

The central phenomenon in psychological illness is dissociation. It involves two complementary aspects: consciousness is at once cut off from
the unconscious and at the same time dominated by it. Dissociation and
possession are inseparable from each other. "Possession by the unconscious means being torn apart into many people and things, a *disiunctio*"
(C.W. 16, par. 397).

It is in relation to possession and disjunction that Jung defined psychosis and neurosis.

Psychosis

It has already been pointed out that Jung first approached psychoanalysis
by way of his day-to-day experience with psychotics. Freud was sensitive
to this and wrote to Jung on August 13, 1908 ". . . to persuade you to
continue my work by applying to psychoses what I have begun with neuroses" (F/J, p. 168).

Jung, however, quickly recognized that repression and the principles
that constitute Freud's topographical model of the psyche were inadequate to explain psychotic experience. "The mechanisms of Freud are
not comprehensive enough to explain why dementia praecox arises and
not hysteria" (C.W. 3, par. 76). In 1911, he wrote to Freud:

> The case is particularly painful because I am now beginning to see what I
> did not see with Honegger. It seems that in Dem. praec. you have at all
> costs to bring to light the inner world produced by the introversion of li-
> bido, which in paranoiacs suddenly appears in distorted form as a delu-
> sional system (Schreber). . . . It seems that introversion leads not only, as
> in hysteria, to a recrudescence of infantile memories but also to a loos-
> ening up of the hysterical layers of the unconscious, thus giving rise to per-
> ilous formations which come to light only in exceptional cases. (F/J, pp.
> 426-7)

Somewhat later, he added, "Mythological parallels are of immense importance for Dementia praecox" (F/J, p. 437).

From this point on, Jung focused his attention on uncovering archaic
dynamics whose eruption in a poorly constituted consciousness produces
psychosis. These dynamics do not take shape in the course of the individual's life. They are, rather, archetypes and belong to the collective
unconscious.

> These contents can be seen most clearly in cases of mental derangement,
> especially in schizophrenia, where mythological images often pour out in

astonishing variety. Insane people frequently produce combinations of ideas and symbols that could never be accounted for by experiences in their individual lives, but only by the history of the human mind. It is an instance of primitive, mythological thinking which reproduces its own primordial images, and is not a reproduction of conscious experiences. (C.W. 8, par. 589)

In many dreams and in certain psychosis we frequently come across archetypal material, i.e., ideas and associations whose exact equivalence can be found in mythology. From these parallels I have drawn the conclusion that there is a layer of the unconscious which functions in exactly the same way as the archaic psyche that produced the myths. (C.W. 17, par. 209)

Jung conceived of psychosis as a state in which fragmentary archetypal organizations erupting in the psyche correlate with deficiencies in the individual psyche. Consciousness is poorly differentiated; and the individual's life circumstances have been unable to foster the formation of a suf - ciently strong personal unconscious. The complexes are loosely structured and the psyche is in a state more characteristic of dream (C.W. 3, par. 557).

Besides recognizing the role of psychogenic deficiencies, Jung always allowed room for the hypothesis of somatic factors in the etiology of psychoses. He asserted his position in 1907 in *Dementia Praecox*, and he repeated it in his last writing on the subject, "Recent Thoughts on Schizophrenia" (1957).

The investigation of schizophrenia is in my view one of the most important tasks for a psychiatry of the future. The problem has two aspects, physiological and psychological, for the disease, so far as we can see today, does not permit of a one-sided explanation. Its symptomatology points on the one hand to an underlying destructive process, possibly of a toxic nature, and on the other—inasmuch as a psychogenic aetiology is not excluded and psychological treatment (in suitable cases) is effective—to a psychic factor of equal importance. Both ways of approach open up far reaching vistas in the theoretical as well as the therapeutic field. (C.W. 3, par. 552)

From the analytic point of view, Jung put forth a hypothesis concerning psychosis, the full implications of which he did not pursue but which eventually proved to be quite productive. According to Jung's hypothesis, psychosis is associated with the anima and animus, while neurosis is associated with the ego complex (C.W. 9/2, par. 40 and par. 62).

Neurosis

Whereas he understood psychosis to be a state within which archaic layers of the unconscious dominate the psyche, Jung understood neurosis as a dissociation of consciousness from the unconscious. Neurosis is a state of disunion from oneself brought about by an opposition between instincts and the imperative needs of civilization, between the will to adapt and infantile capriciousness, and between individual and collective duties.

> The point is that most neuroses are misdevelopments that have been built up over many years, and these cannot be remedied by a short and intensive process. (C.W. 16, par. 36)

> Neuroses, like all illnesses, are symptoms of maladjustment. Because of some obstacle—a constitutional weakness or defect, wrong education, bad experiences, and unsuitable attitude, etc.—one shrinks from the difficulties which life brings and thus finds oneself back in the world of the infant. . . . (C.W. 13, par. 473)

While remaining in a regressed state, the neurotic personality makes choices that tear it from its roots.

> A neurosis makes itself known when we adopt a behavior that does not overcome within us the primitive vertebrate and animal that cling to the sympathetic nervous system. (H.D.A., p. 351, tr. RGJ)

> A neurosis results when one fails to recognize and strays from the fundamental laws of the living body. (H.D.A., p. 352, tr. RGJ)

With respect to the four personality functions, neurosis suggests a one-sided development. The personality makes use of some functions while it neglects others.

> Those sharp cleavages and antagonisms between conscious and unconscious, such as we see so clearly in the endless conflicts of neurotic natures, nearly always rest on a noticeable one-sidedness of the conscious attitude, which gives absolute precedence to one or two functions, while the others are unjustly thrust into the background. Conscious realization and experiences of fantasies assimilate the unconscious inferior functions to the conscious mind—a process which is naturally not without far-reaching effects on the conscious attitudes. (C.W. 17, par. 359)

Finally, Jung insisted upon the social dimension of neurosis.

> A neurosis is more a psychosocial phenomenon than an illness in the strict sense. It forces us to extend the term "illness" beyond the idea of an individual body whose functions are disturbed, and to look upon the neurotic person as a sick system of social relationships. (C.W. 16, par. 27)

Apperception and Attitude

Two factors play a particularly important role in neurosis because they contribute to shaping the relationship of consciousness with the unconscious. These two factors are apperception and attitude.

The concepts of apperception are those categories that consciousness uses to understand what happens to it.

> This explains numerous neurotic disturbances which arise from the fact
> that certain contents are constellated in the unconscious but cannot be as-
> similated owing to the lack of apperceptive concepts that would "grasp"
> them. (C.W. 9/2, par. 259)

Apperceptive concepts make up the culture within which conscious-ness first learned to function. If these concepts are indispensable for re-ceiving whatever arises from the unconscious, they are nevertheless of a collective nature and are therefore inadequate to account for the individ-ual's potential and destiny. At a profound level, individuals are necessar-ily in conflict with their culture and with the type of normalcy that it imposes.

> Consequently there are just as many people who become neurotic because
> they are merely normal, as there are people who are neurotic because they
> cannot become normal. (C.W. 16, par. 161)

> But anyone who attempts to do both, to adjust to his group and at the
> same time pursue his individual goal, becomes neurotic. (M.D.R., p. 344)

Above and beyond the categories of apperception, it is therefore the conscious attitude that is in question. Jung insisted upon the determina-tive role of what he called *Einstellung* (accommodation, the focusing of an optical apparatus) and *Betrachtungsweise* (manner of considering). Un-conscious dynamics are neither good nor bad; they behave according to the attitude one takes towards them.

> The constellation of archetypal images and fantasies is not in itself patho-
> logical. The pathological element consists in the way individual conscious-
> ness interprets and reacts to the constellation. (G.W. 9/1, par. 261, tr.
> RGJ)

An inappropriate attitude engenders a bad form, in the sense Gestalt theory uses the term "form"; and the phenomenon tends to deteriorate into a vicious circle.

> The hero motif is invariably accompanied by the dragon motif; the dragon
> and the hero who fights him are two figures of the same myth. (C.W. 18,
> par. 191)

The conscious attitude depends on complexes. A change of conscious attitude cannot come about simply through reflection or volition. But it is therapeutically important to begin with this conscious attitude if one is to avoid setting off the analysand's resistances. Jung wrote the following about this issue:

Freud makes his theory of neurosis—so admirably suited to the nature of neurotics—much too dependent on the neurotic ideas from which precisely the patients suffer. This leads to the pretense (which suits the neurotic down to the ground) that the *causa efficiens* of his neurosis lies in the remote past. In reality the neurosis is manufactured anew every day, with the help of a false attitude that consists in the neurotic's thinking and feeling as he does and justifying it by his theory of neurosis. (C.W. 5, par. 655)

The Meaning of Illness

Psychic disturbances are neither symptoms to be eradicated nor dysfunctions to be normalized. Jung is far from advocating the idea that a patient's speech needs to be pulled apart and reorganized. In contradiction to all normative visions, Jung believed that it is sometimes necessary to shield the patient from the therapist's convictions and that no theory can presume to know a person's fate.

> He [the therapist] should remember that the patient is there to be treated and not to verify a theory. (C.W. 16, par. 237)

Far from seeking to eliminate symptoms, treatment actually depends on them. The personal history of the patient is ". . . the patient's secret, the rock against which he is shattered. If I know his secret story, I have a key to the treatment" (M.D.R., p. 117). Symptoms express simultaneously the disorders of the psyche and the correctives, or the compensatory dynamics that the unconscious attempts to bring to these disorders. Symptoms also announce that psychic energy has been activated.

> Certainly the unconscious is not always and in all circumstances dangerous, but as soon as a neurosis is present it is a sign of a special heaping up of energy in the unconscious, like a charge that may explode. (C.W. 7, par. 192)

> In the intensity of the emotional disturbance itself lies the value, the energy which he should have at his disposal in order to remedy the state of reduced adaptation. (C.W. 8, par. 166)

Illness is part and parcel of the subject's history. No original state exists to which one can return and from which one can start life over again; nor is there an Apollonian psyche that one can dream of ever reaching. History is inexorable. It does not turn backwards. Subjects are constituted both when they accept themselves as they are and when they make an effort to free and integrate the creative dynamics that are active in the illnesses afflicting them.

> The purely causalistic approach is too narrow and fails to do justice to the true significance either of the dream or of the neurosis. (C.W. 16, par. 307)

It is within the neuroses that the values the subject lacks can be found. (H.D.A., p. 101ff., tr. RGJ)

In Jung's view, the original state is present in one's current life in a two-fold way. First, the past is accessible only by means of the psyche's present; that is, the past is transformed, symbolized, and framed in the context of the present. Second, the original state is the ever-present source of archetypal information to which therapeutic regression must be allowed to return. There are therefore two modes of regression: one toward past events and their symbolization in the present, the other toward archetypal patterns and their representations.

And if, finally, neurotic symptoms appear, then the attitude of consciousness, its ruling idea, is contradicted, and in the unconscious there is a stirring up of those archetypes that were the most suppressed by the conscious attitude. The therapist then has no other course than to confront the ego with its adversary and thus initiate the melting and recasting process. (C.W. 14, par. 505)

The Therapeutic Intention

Keeping in mind that the subject's achievements surpass those of the ego, Jung defined analysis as the process whereby the subject acquires an identity (C.W. 11, par. 884). This venture is set in motion by each patient's psychic illness or wound, for it is these that really call the condition of the subject into question. For this reason, no subject can enter analysis without distorting the experience if he or she is motivated by the desire for power, culture, or a language. Nor can analysis be made into the systematic application of one particular understanding of human nature. It is and remains motivated by therapeutic intention because it seeks the meaning of the psychic wounds it attempts to heal. But analysis is not, however, a cure—a treatment limited to making symptoms disappear. It embraces the full scope of each person's destiny as well as relationships to the world and to oneself.

Analysis can be seen as the equivalent of an initiation for the Western mind. It pursues self-knowledge (C.W. 11, par. 854) and unfolds through a dual activity allowing the most profound unconscious dynamics to speak and permitting one to become conscious of others and of oneself.

Therapy aims at strengthening the conscious mind. . . . (C.W. 16, par. 479)

Here one may ask, perhaps, why is it so desirable that a man should be individuated. Not only is it desirable, it is absolutely indispensable because, through his contamination with others, he falls into situations and commits actions which bring him into disharmony with himself. From all states of unconscious contamination and non-differentiation there is begotten a compulsion to be and to act in a way contrary to one's nature. Accordingly, a man can neither be at one with himself nor accept responsibility for himself. (C.W. 7, par. 373)

Self-awareness is sterile if it does not go hand-in-hand with a living relationship to the sources of what makes us human, a personal relationship that takes shape within an attitude and within symbols that are the subject's own.

However involved in analytic therapy and however convinced of its efficacy, Jung was nonetheless courageous enough to dispel an illusion that some insist upon preserving:

[T]he principal aim of psychotherapy is not to transport the patient to an impossible state of happiness, but to help him acquire steadfastness and philosophic patience in face of suffering. Life demands for its completion and fulfillment a balance between joy and sorrow. (C.W. 16, par. 185)

Science and Myth

Those readers who were already familiar with Jung's works before opening this book perhaps have not found what they were expecting. Where is the pastor's son who, throughout life, understood himself in the light of the Christian tradition? Where is the psychiatrist? Where is the man who had a passion for alchemical imagery, or who discerned the dynamics of opposites operative within different social and cultural spheres of life? And in a more personal way, I would like to ask: Where is the old fisherman of Lake Zürich?

My purpose has been to tease out the internal logic of Jung's multifarious work, not to write about the circumstances surrounding it nor to discuss its various theses. I remain within these limits as I conclude.

The major fact with which Jung's work confronts us is the living relationship between consciousness and the unconscious.

Unconscious dynamics are not the result of repression only, nor do they arise merely in counterpart to the formation of the subject. Some of these unconscious dynamics sustain and organize the human condition. They are the ground of therapeutic hope. If they are at the origins of psychic disturbances, they can also be sources of reparation and growth whenever consciousness enters into an appropriate relationship with them.

> A complete "emptying" of the unconscious is out of the question, if only because its creative powers are continually producing new formations. Consciousness, no matter how extensive it may be, must always remain the smaller circle within the greater circle of the unconscious, an island surrounded by the sea; and, like the sea itself, the unconscious yields an endless and self-replenishing abundance of living creatures, a wealth beyond our fathoming. (C.W. 16, par. 366)

The task of becoming conscious is essential to life. It is up to consciousness to draw out what is potential, to "ex-press" it, to put it into
words. Without consciousness nothing can take shape. Jung saw in this
conscious process the meaning of his own existence (M.D.R., p. 287).

Becoming conscious is not only a matter of gaining understanding. A
conscious awareness of projections reveals the self-alienation of the personality and tears apart the identifications that constitute the personality. The resulting conflict puts into motion a profound transformation.
The person who disengages from such a conflict is structured by a polarity comprised of two fields, one conscious and the other unconscious.
The former is enclosed within the limits that social life imposes, the latter has a connection to the sources of unconscious information.

This evolution, whose orientation and interplay are recognizable today, is neither simple nor assured.

> Everything in the unconscious seeks outward manifestation, and the per-
> sonality too desires to evolve out of its unconscious conditions and to ex-
> perience itself as a whole. (M.D.R., p. 3)

> There is within man a deeply rooted resistance to everything that would
> allow him to know more about himself. This is why inner development
> does not always follow with increased external knowledge and activities.
> (G.W. VIII, par. 191, tr. RGJ)

> Hence all unconscious nature longs for the light of consciousness while
> franctically struggling against it all the same. (C.W. 11, par. 745)

Jungian analysis is an exercise in contradictions. This is why a number
of those who comment upon Jung's works miss the mark and distort his
ideas. They simplify and systematize because they still confuse philosophical positivism with scientific rigor. They cannot think using a scheme
that simultaneously maintains and goes beyond the opposition between
matter and spirit, the rational and the non-rational, or representation
and reality. To understand Jung's thought, one must make use of multiple approaches.

When Jung said that the psychological point of view is that of the
"knower of divine secrets" (*Erkenner göttlicher Geheimnisse*) (C.W. 11,
par. 430), the reader is astounded by the mixture of psychology and mys-
ticism in this statement. Jung had no intention of confusing these two.
He meant to say that whoever approaches psychic phenomena and experiences a feeling of mystery stands a better chance of perceiving their importance and truth. Jung goes beyond the schism between the positivist
reduction of psychology and the metaphysical projection of religion,

and he does so in order to apprehend the psyche in its full scope and intensity.

In the face of psychic reality, Jung applied himself to the task of putting into place an epistemology that does not diminish the irrational and yet somehow allows reason to apprehend it. He considered scientific effort to be an essential part of the process of becoming conscious.

> I saw that so much fantasy needed firm ground under foot, and that I must return wholly to reality. For me, reality meant scientific comprehension. I had to draw concrete conclusions from the insights the unconscious had given me—and that task was to become a life work. (M.D.R., p. 188)

> I regard my concepts as suggestions and attempts at the formulation of a new scientific psychology based in the first place upon immediate experience with human beings. (I.P., p. IX, tr. RGJ)

But science left to its own devices cannot express what is human. Knowledge comes about not only by means of a rational elaboration; it also requires myth. The history of the sciences is imbued with the unconscious, and for each age and society, thoughts and images whose origins are unknown have been the representations of meaning that has made life possible. Jung had no illusion about the dangers of myth, but he had the courage to recognize its role.

> Cut off the intermediary world of mythic imagination, and the mind falls prey to doctrinaire rigidities. On the other hand, too much traffic with these germs of myth is dangerous for weak and suggestible minds, for they are led to mistake vague intimations for substantial knowledge, and to hypostatize mere phantasms. (M.D.R., p. 316)

> The more the critical reason dominates, the more impoverished life becomes; but the more of the unconscious, and the more of myth we're capable of making conscious, the more of life we integrate. Overvalued reason has this in common with political absolutism: under its dominion the individual is pauperized. (M.D.R., p. 302).

Bibliography of Elie Humbert's Writings in Analytical Psychology

1971   "La Question du Sens." *Planète Plus*, special issue on Jung. Translated into German under the title, "Die Frage nach der Sinn," in *Zeitschrift für Analytische Psychologie un Ihre frey gebiete*, second year, Vol. 3.

"Active Imagination—Theory and Practice." *Spring*.

1974   "Image et Réalité du Soi d'après C.G. Jung." *Cahiers de Psychologie Jungienne*, No. 1, printemps, and No. 2, été.

"Le Concept d'Ombre." *Cahiers de Psychologie Jungienne*, No. 3, automne.

1975   "Inceste et Ouroboros." With Geneviève Guy-Gillet. *Cahiers de Psychologie Jungienne*, No. 5, printemps.

"L'Expérience Onirique." *Revue de Psychologie et des Sciences de l'Education*. Université de Louvain. Vol. 11, Nos. 2–3.

"Conditions d'une Symbolique Clinique." *Cahiers de Psychologie Jungienne*, No. 7, 3ième trimestre.

1976   "Réflections sur la Dépression." *Cahiers de Psychologie Jungienne*, No. 8, hiver.

"Anima/Animus." *Cahiers de Psychologie Jungienne*, No. 11, automne.

1977   "L'Imagination Active d'après C.G. Jung." *Cahiers de Psychologie Jungienne*, No. 13, printemps. Translated into English in *Jung in Modern Perspective*, edited by R. Papadopoulos. Wilwood House Ltd.; Hounslow, 1984.

Definitions of Jung's analytic terms in *Vocabulaire des Psychothérapies*, edited by A. Virel. Fayard; Paris.

1978   "L'Expérience Onirique." Revision of 1975 article in *Cahiers de Psychologie Jungienne*, No. 16, hiver.

1978   "Kairos—le Moment—Différents Vécus de l'Expérience du Centre."
       Cahiers de Psychologie Jungienne, No. 18, septembre.

1979   "Réflections sur les Idées d'Archétype et d'Inconscient Collectif." *Cahiers
       de Psychologie Jungienne*, No. 21, 2ième trimestre.

       "Le Soi et le Narcissisme—Réflections Préalables." *Cahiers de Psychologie
       Jungienne*, No. 22, 3ième trimestre. Translated as "The Self and Narcis-
       sism" in the *Journal of Analytical Psychology*, 1980, Vol. 23, No. 4.

       "Il Ruolo dell'Immagine nella Psychologia Analitica" in *Parole e Immagine
       Strumenti dell'Analisi*. Edited by E. Raffei. Marsilio, No. 20.

1980   "La Prise du Symbole." *Cahiers de Psychologie Jungienne*, No. 25.

       "Une Pratique du Sens." *Science et Conscience*. Stock; Paris.

       "Introduction à la Troisième Journée." *Science et Conscience*. Stock; Paris.

       "Active Imagination Questioned and Discussed." *Methods of Treatment
       in Analytical Psychology*. Ed. by Ian F. Baker. Bonz; Fellbach.

1982   "Des Organisateurs Inconscients—L'Idée d'Archetype selon C.G. Jung."
       Cahiers de Psychologie Jungienne, No. 32.

       "Jung et l'Interrogation Réligieuse." *Cahiers de Psychologie Jungienne*,
       No. 34. Translated in Spring 1985.

       "Un Parcours Analytique de 79 à 87." *Etudes Psychothérapiques*, 13ième
       Année, No. 1, No. 47.

       "Le Discours du Rêve." *Etudes Psychothérapiques*, 13ième Année, No. 1,
       No. 49.

1983   "Le Soi à l'Epreuve d'un Groupe de Travail—Avant-Propos." *Cahiers de
       Psychologie Jungienne*, No. 39.

       "L'Interprétation des Rêves et leurs Contenus." *La Serrure et le Songe*,
       edited by Prof. Pelicier. Editions Economica, Coll. Medea.

1984   "Inconscient Collectif et Désir Infantile." *Cahiers de Psychologie Jungienne*,
       No. 42.

       "Le Merveilleux." Study in the form of conclusion in *Le Merveilleux—
       L'Imaginaire et les Croyances en Occident*. Edited by Michel Merlin. Bordas;
       Paris.

1985   "La Question du Sens." Revised and corrected version of 1971a. *Perpectives
       Psychiatriques*, 23ième Année, No. 101.

1986   "Le Puits de la Mémoire." *Cahiers de Psychologie Jungienne*, No. 49.

       "Unité et/ou Integrité." *Approches du Réel*. Edited by M.-O. Monchicourt.
       The Tsukuba Colloquium. Editions du Mail.

Index